NO SMALL
MIRACLES

HEARTWARMING, HUMOROUS
& HOPEFILLED STORIES FROM A
PEDIATRIC CHAPLAIN

NORRIS BURKES

INTEGRITY®
PUBLISHERS
Nashville

No Small Miracles

Published by Integrity Publishers, a division of Integrity Media, Inc., 5250 Virginia Way, Suite 110, Brentwood, TN 37027.

Helping people worldwide experience *the* manifest presence *of* God.

Cover Design: Kirk DouPonce, DogEaredDesign.com
Cover Photograph: Stephen Gardner, ShootPW.com
Interior Design: Inside Out Design & Typesetting

Names and details in some of the stories in this volume may have been changed to protect the subjects' privacy.

In 2004, several essays included in this volume earned third-place honors in each of three national writing contests: the general interest category for the National Society of Newspaper Columnists, the Cornell Award from the Religion Newswriter's Association, and the Amy Foundation, which sponsors a program recognizing "creative, skillful writing that presents in a sensitive, thought-provoking manner the biblical position on issues affecting the world today."

For more information about the author, go to www.thechaplain.net or www.chaplainnorris.com.

Library of Congress Cataloging-in-Publication Data

Burkes, Norris.
  No small miracles / by Norris Burkes.
    p. cm.
Summary: "Heartwarming and courageous stories of those who have faced difficult life situations in hospital emergencies"—Provided by publisher.

ISBN-13: 9-781-59145-425-0
ISBN-10: 1-59145-425-5 (hardcover)

  1. Hospital patients—Religious life—Case studies.   I. Title.
BV4910.B87   2006
248.8'611–dc22   2005036458

Printed in the United States of America
06 07 08 09 10 11 BVG 9 8 7 6 5 4 3 2 1

To Roger, my lifelong friend.
This book is dedicated to you and your struggle with—
and victory over—
a double bout of cancer.

CONTENTS

Acknowledgments   vii

Introduction: Discovering the Real Miracles   1

Part 1. **Parents, Prayers, and Miracles in the Pediatric Unit**   7

A Tiny Handful of Promise ○ *A Child's Cries Translate to Prayers* ○ *Evidence of Things Hoped For* ○ *Eighty Minutes of Parenting* ○ *The Prayers of Beginning* ○ *The Gift* ○ *"Where Is My Child?"* ○ *Dear Adriana, . . .* ○ *One More Breath* ○ *Burdens Too Great* ○ *Do You See What I See?* ○ *Alicia's Feet . . . and Her Father's Hands* ○ *Without Grace, It's a Small World* ○ *An Unusual Ring to the Day* ○ *A Candy Bar Blessing*

Part 2. **"Chaplain to the ER, Stat!"**   53

Every Available Response ○ *It Takes a Child to Raise a Village* ○ *Suicide—a Rafting Trip into White-Water Tears* ○ *In the Twinkling of an Eye* ○ *The Cost of Love* ○ *The Houseguest* ○ *A Delicate Balance*

Part 3.   Grown-Up Miracles   77

Distractions Cloud Purpose ○ *Lip-Sync Prayers* ○ *Unimaginable News* ○ *Making Mama Cry* ○ *A Miracle in the Input, if Not in the Outcome* ○ *The Bravest Words* ○ *The Language of the Eyes*

Part 4.   Miracles in Uniform   99

The Dance ○ *The Soldier's Gethsemane Moment* ○ *A Delay of Sacred Remembrance* ○ *So You Think You're a Stud!* ○ *The Dreaded Knock on the Door* ○ *Promotion on a Different Level*

Part 5.   Miracles on the Home Front:
**   The Personal Life of a Chaplain**   121

"I Take Thee, Norris" ○ *Don't Ask My Wife to Pray for You!* ○ *A Son's Tumble, a Father's Tears* ○ *Cast Your Vote* ○ *My World, Turned Upside Down* ○ *Unbalanced Parenting* ○ *Why Must I Ask for a Miracle—Again?* ○ *Hearts Soften in a Small Bed* ○ *Search and Rescue in Wal-Mart* ○ *Faith Wavers in the Dentist's Chair* ○ *Are You My Daughter?* ○ *Falling to the Obvious Conclusion* ○ *A Good Marriage Requires Sweat* ○ *Church Hopping* ○ *Seeing Both Sides of Beauty* ○ *Just When We Need It, a Laugh* ○ *Almost Helping* ○ *Grief Comes to the Grief Counselor* ○ *A Tough Week for Fathers* ○ *Regretting a Moment . . . for a Lifetime* ○ *When the Lights Go Out* ○ *What Legacy Will You Leave?*

ACKNOWLEDGMENTS

In 2001, when I was forty-four years old, people started telling me something I truthfully found unbelievable. They started telling me they thought I had a gift for writing.

At first I denied that writing could possibly be my gift. I likened the possibility to finding a million dollars that had fallen off an armored truck. In the analogy, I try to return the money, but people keep insisting it belongs to me. "Really, it's yours," they insist. "Keep it."

Thankfully, I finally recognized this gift, and eventually I found it to be a salvation, a resurrection of my spirit, a guide that brought me into the clearing where I could see my way.

But I didn't find it on my own; many people were willing to be my guide along the way, and I gratefully acknowledge their help.

To the readers of my syndicated newspaper column: Thank you for your interest and your feedback. And a special thanks to the readers of *Florida Today* newspaper who've been with me since the beginning. Thanks for your unrelenting encouragement (and sometimes nagging) to write this book.

To my friends on the *Florida Today* staff: Tom, thanks for trusting me with a space in your paper. Suzy, Dee, and the editing team, thanks for holding my hand when I was insecure and holding my feet to the fire about attributing sources. Bob, and especially your wife, Jane, thanks for seeing the heart of the column.

To my agent, Kathleen: Much gratitude to you for trying "just one more publisher."

To the folks at Integrity Publishers, Joey, Sue Ann, and the others: Thanks for your vision for this book!

To Joel: You dared to dream for me. Congratulations to you and Laura!

To all my wonderful friends and colleagues at the Sutter Medical Center in Sacramento, and my friends and former co-workers at the Houston Northwest Medical Center and the University of California Davis Medical Center in Sacramento, three places where many of these stories took place: What a privilege it has been for me to work among such talented and dedicated professionals.

To my volunteer proofreaders, Alan, Ed, Deborah, Marcetta, Kim, and Davalynn: Thanks for checking my grammar, my syntax, and my common sense.

To my mom, Dolores: Thanks for teaching me good grammar so my proofreaders weren't too overwhelmed.

To Chaplain Tamara, the unwitting co-writer of many of my columns: While your name is not on the cover of this book, it will always be written across the depth of my gratitude.

To Jason Fontaine of Inkblot Studio: Your great Web design and careful archiving of my columns were essential to the writing of this book.

To Wil and Darla, my biggest fans (probably because I write a lot about Wil's firstborn): Thanks for rearing a wonderful daughter.

And to that firstborn, Becky, my wife and best friend: You have been the good-natured subject of many of my writings. Twenty-six years ago, when the volunteer at the polling place asked you, "Is he always that funny?" you knew the truth. You knew about my dark places; nevertheless you've stayed. From the dark places my writing has sent me to—and from which it has lifted me—you have always been there. I love you eternally.

And to our children, Sara, Michael, Brittney, and Nicole: Thank you for your good-natured willingness to be the subject of so many of these columns. (And no, Mike, you can't have a cut.)

Introduction:
Discovering the Real Miracles

In an impatient tone that fell short of her namesake quality, Grace, a nurse in the intensive care unit, asked tersely, "Chaplain, what are you doing at 2 p.m.?"

"Uh . . ." Caught off guard, my afternoon schedule suddenly vanished from my memory. As chaplain for a Houston hospital in the early 1990s, my days stayed pretty full; but at that moment, I couldn't remember what I was doing in the next minute, let alone several hours later.

"We have an end-of-life conference with a family. Can you make it?" Frustrated by the lengthy use of an ICU bed, Grace had called the conference to discuss continuing life support for a seventy-five-year-old male stroke victim who had shown no sign of brain activity for sixty days.

"Life support" is a misnomer. At times like this, it should be called "mechanical maintenance." This man wasn't being *supported*; he was being *preserved*. Yet despite those efforts, his body was literally decaying. Typically, most TV-watching Americans describe the process of discontinuing life support as "pulling the plug." They picture a nurse grimly yanking twenty tubes from every orifice or throwing a big switch somewhere that turns off all the electronic apparatuses, sending the patient's room into a quiet hush except for the flatline hum of the monitor. Actually, it's far less dramatic, involving the slow turning of a few knobs. Done properly, it's usually a peaceful process.

When this family showed up in the conference room, it was quickly apparent that their hearts weren't anywhere near ready for our discussion. This family was "claiming a miracle." They didn't care what anyone said. They were claiming that their father would rise from his deathbed in three days. That was their definition of a miracle, defined and customized.

Shifting the conversation, I asked them what it might be like if they redefined what a miracle meant in this situation. What would a miracle look like, I asked, if they allowed the frame to be removed from their picture of God—if they accepted that the mysterious and unlimited workings of God might produce a miracle that differed from the one they had in mind?

Consider Jesus' example, and you'll see that even he was sometimes uncomfortable with the use of miracles. He didn't intend them as something that would prove the existence of God. He told one group of scoffers that even if he were to raise someone from the dead, they still wouldn't believe. The fact is, we may learn as much from studying Jesus' *avoidance* of miracles on certain occasions as we do by reading how and when he did perform them. For instance, at Calvary he was taunted by people who demanded that he come down from the cross. "He saved others," they sneered, "but he can't save himself!" (Matthew 27:42). It never occurred to them that a miracle was occurring even his closest followers couldn't see (although Jesus had told them it would happen).

Like those disciples, we, too, often overlook the real miracles. Maybe, while we're waiting and watching for one preconceived miracle to happen, something else happens but we fail to see the miraculous in it.

For instance, maybe the true miracle isn't always going to be that Dad survives cancer but that his prodigal children come back into his life. Perhaps the real miracle will not be a baby's survival after a difficult birth but that somehow she will introduce a presence of God to her family or even to hospital staff.

Miracles aren't always about getting something back; sometimes they are about finding a fuller appreciation for what you have left when that something is taken away. Maybe the true miracle isn't always going to be about saving the world but about gaining new appreciation for a piece of it.

During the week following the end-of-life conference (in which the family did finally agree to discontinue life support), I saw at least two miracles. That father didn't walk out of our hospital, no, but three sisters found agreement in prayer as they united at their father's bedside and gave him permission to walk into the arms of a waiting God. That was the first miracle. And the second and more lasting miracle was that the sisters discovered an infinite God whom they could not control.

And in my experience, knowing a God whom you cannot control is the first step toward knowing that God is in control.

REDEFINING MIRACLES

This book is about miracles, and I've written it for two reasons. First, I want you to redefine your concept of what a miracle is in hopes you'll watch for and discover the real miracles that occur in your life. Much of the time when we pray for miracles, we specify just how that miracle will unfold: "Help Jimmy walk again, Lord." "Give Daddy back his sight." "Make Mama whole again, Jesus!" But it seems to me that miracles, by their very definition, are *not* what we think they will be. They are something wholly (and holy!) different.

The stories in this book are about people I have encountered in my current work as a hospital chaplain—primarily now assigned to pediatric and women's units but also working in other areas of the hospital as well—and also in my work as a military chaplain. We'll start with stories I've heard—or lived through—in the hospital setting. Then we'll move on to military "miracles." Since 1986, I have worn the uniform of the United States Air Force as both a reserve chaplain and, for eight years, as an active duty chaplain. Now, as I approach retirement from military service, I want to share some of the insights and lessons I've learned from the brave men and women who serve our country.

Those depicted in these stories are, for the most part, colleagues, friends, or patients and their families—people I met in my hospital work or in the military—who faced unexpected, and in some cases unspeakable, challenges and tragedies and who saw God do a different thing than they expected or could have imagined. In most cases, they might have prayed for big miracles but instead experienced small ones that gave new meaning to their lives. Perhaps a life was lost, but a heart was softened. Maybe a disease wasn't cured, but a relationship was restored.

The other reason I wrote this book was to answer a question. For years people have asked me, "How do you do it?"

"It" refers to my job as a chaplain.

The truth is that chaplaincy is the most rewarding ministry I have ever done in my twenty-five years of ordained life. So, to explain how I do my job and also to share with you the rewards inherent in this work, I've written these stories. In this book, I hope to unwrap the lessons and dislodge the miracles that might otherwise be missed.

Being a chaplain means I have been privileged to hear stories few others would hear. As part of an interdisciplinary team, I was obliged to share those stories with other caregivers when it meant that patient care could be enhanced. Now, several years later, I share those stories with you, hoping they might also enhance *your* life and give depth to your ability to care for others.

But I must warn you, it is the drama in these stories that makes them memorable—and contagious. Some of them may be hard to read; I completely understand. In the beginning days of my hospital ministry, there were many nights when I lay awake, wondering whether my loved ones or I might become the subject of one of these dramatic stories. I'd imagine my children in a car crash. Or I'd wonder if my back pain might be the onset of a failing kidney. In fact, on one night my imagination conjured up enough chest pain to convince the nursing supervisor I should be admitted for overnight observation. (I somehow doubt that the nurses on that Houston telemetry unit will ever forget seeing the south end of their chaplain going north down that corridor.)

Over the years, however, my worries eventually eased, and I began to see the overall thread of the divine presence woven through the lives entangled with tragedies. I began to see miracles again and again. In these pages—and in your life—I hope you'll see them too.

Part 1

Parents, Prayers, and Miracles in the Pediatric Unit

After you've run bowlegged behind your children as they learn to ride a two-wheeled bike . . . After you've helped them study for their learner's permit—and after you've ridden bravely in the passenger seat . . .

After you've seen them off on their first date and sat up late, waiting for them to get home . . .

After you've sat for hours on rusty bleachers on a sweltering afternoon, waiting to hear your child's name called as the soccer team runs onto the field . . .

After you've shivered on freezing football nights, praying your son will get up again when a too-hard tackle knocked him down . . .

After each step of your children's lives, you hope and pray that God has another miracle coming that will eventually launch them into the world of their dreams. Those are the routine prayers, the confident requests we all make as moms and dads.

But in the hospital, parents' prayers are different. They echo urgently down the hallways of every pediatric unit in every hospital. Usually they are not prayers for small miracles; often they are prayers that seek results exceeding the greatest of million-to-one odds.

As a pediatric chaplain who also works in the labor and delivery department, I hear a lot of prayers, especially the prayers of parents. These prayers connect our young patients to the very beginnings and roots of who they are and why they are.

In many ways, parents' prayers are the prayers of our Creator. Overhearing and sharing in these prayers, I often see miracles occur—if not in the outcome of their family's situation, then in the workings of their hearts as they reconnect with him.

A TINY HANDFUL OF PROMISE

It was 3 a.m. when the doctors flooded her room with light. Still numb from pain medication, the new mom fumbled for her glasses, squinting to distinguish the blur of white coats. The doctors were saying something about needing some papers signed—*now*.

Twenty miles and twenty minutes away, a high-pitched beep suddenly filled my dark bedroom. Numb from the early hour, I fumbled for my glasses, too, so I could read the number on my pager. "Oh no, it's too early," I groaned, even as I shuffled toward the closet where I had pre-positioned my clothing. Still groggy, I managed to get dressed while placing a whispered phone call to the maternity ward.

"Chaplain, we have a baby who's not doing well," the nurse reported. "The parents are asking for you to please come."

Maternity wards are the happiest places on earth—except when they are the saddest places on earth. The contrast in patient stories on the floor can be jagged and capricious. Even as I enter a room of sobbing parents, I often will glance over my shoulder to see other families happily backslapping each other with congratulatory pats.

As I stepped to the bedside, the couple told me of their journey through a problem pregnancy filled with frightening neonatal reports. Nevertheless, they had nursed thin hopes that doctors would find things more fixable than predicted. But now the baby had arrived, and initial reports showed underdeveloped lungs and a leaky heart that was beginning to fail. Concerned doctors were seeking parental consent for a birth-day surgery.

"Has God just teased us?" the parents wondered aloud. "What do we have to do? How do we pray? What do we say? Would it help to baptize the baby? Can you baptize her, Chaplain? Or bless her? Something. We've got to do something! She's got to have a chance."

Now, you have to understand: in my tradition I don't baptize babies. But those who would argue theology at a time like this have never looked into the eyes of desperate parents and heard them say, "Do something, Chaplain!"

I asked the mother if she might have the strength to come with me to the neonatal intensive care unit (the NICU, which staffers pronounce "nick-u"). The NICU is a world of wires, IV bottles, tubes, and back-lit beds that remind me of the scene in the movie *E.T.* when scores of scientists and doctors examine the little alien. In close quarters, the doctors, nurses, and respiratory therapists squeeze through tangled tubes to deliver highly spe- cialized health care to the tiniest people you'll ever see. But as cramped as it was in there, the staff made room as I entered with parents and two sets of grandparents in tow. As we encircled the baby, the usually noisy NICU fell silent in readiness for this "emergency blessing."

Mom stood beside her tiny daughter, stroking the baby with her index finger in an attempt to reestablish the sustaining love of the umbilical cord. Her finger seemed just long enough to main- tain a fragile connection between her and this baby of faith. It was an image reminiscent of the fingertip touch between God and Adam in Michelangelo's painting in the Sistine Chapel.

In the *E.T.* movie, special-effects artisans attempted to recreate the scene using an extraterrestrial with a flashlight finger to deliver a healing touch to a child, but Hollywood could never paint *this* scene. Yet it is a scene that is enacted every day in our special-care nursery.

Here was a mother trying to give her very breath to a child who could only breathe with a machine. With the touch of a single finger, Mom was sharing the hopes and prayers of a family.

Unceremoniously opening a bottle of sterile water, I placed a drop on the baby's forehead and asked that God "bless this child in the name of the Father, Son, and Holy Spirit."

With that, Mom's whimpers melted into weeping. And as she cried, she took her daughter's tiny hand and, finding a spot that wasn't wrapped, poked, or monitored, she placed a kiss in that tiny palm and whispered something into those little, curled-up fingers. Then, as if she had placed a thing of priceless value in her daughter's grip for safekeeping, she closed it tight.

This mother's love reminded me of the miraculous way in which God whispers his love into the hand of each of us when we are born, placing there a promise that, no matter what, he will never let us go. And having pledged that love to us from our first breath to our last, he wraps our fingers around that promise for safekeeping.

The apostle Paul wrote, "For I am persuaded, that neither death, nor life, nor angels, nor principalities, nor powers, nor things present, nor things to come, nor height, nor depth, nor any other creature, shall be able to separate us from the love of God, which is in Christ Jesus our Lord" (Romans 8:38–39 KJV). Even as a minister, I sometimes forget how personal and deep God's love is for each of us. I often talk about the depth of God's love, but it took a mother's heartfelt whisper into a tiny hand to remind me that God is always there to love me, and all I need to do is reach out and accept it.

I'll never know the exact words this young mother entrusted to her daughter's grip. But in the coming weeks of miraculous procedures and risky surgeries, the real miracle that was witnessed by all who would see it was how this little girl never released the grip of her mother's promise.

Three months after her birth, she went home a healthy little girl.

A CHILD'S CRIES TRANSLATE TO PRAYERS

Few of us have the patience to tolerate a child's fit of screaming. Mostly it's mothers who hear the cries of a child as a prayer to be quickly answered.

Yet recently in our presurgery unit, it wasn't the cries of the child that were noticed by a fellow patient, but rather the lack of his cries. Looking across from another gurney at the seven-month-old boy, the woman patient gushed, "He's so cute and so well mannered."

"Well mannered?" I asked, looking at her through squinted eyes.

"Yes, he's been poked all morning, yet he's not let out a peep of protest."

She paused, searching my expression for a clue. "But I know you can't tell me anything. I understand."

I smiled.

"Really I do."

No, she didn't. The more she said she understood, the more all hope of understanding departed from her.

The fact was that the baby, born prematurely, was having surgery because he couldn't scream. He couldn't cry. He couldn't coo. He couldn't sigh. It was his third surgery, and each one was bringing him closer to the day when he would voice a cry of praise (or protest) that would be welcomed by all who loved him.

Meanwhile, in a room six floors up, a little boy was demonstrating that he had enough lung power for the two of them. The boy had experienced a painful three years since his own premature birth, and that morning his shrieks had driven his grandmother from the room.

In an adjoining waiting area, I found her staring into the cloudless California afternoon as she, too, cried torrents of tears.

"I'm the pediatric chaplain," I said, stepping into the room.

"I know I should be in there with my grandson, but I couldn't stand hearing . . ." She placed a hand over her mouth to mute her own cries.

"It's OK," I interrupted. "It must be hard to hear."

"He's had so many procedures, he can hardly stand to see anyone in a white coat. Right now they're in there looking for another vein to poke. But," she added, casting a glance toward the quiet room opposite her grandson's, "I guess I should be glad he can cry at all."

The spiritual frequency being monitored by this loving grandmother was not only picking up the vocal screams of her grandson but, as I was about to learn, another boy's silent screams as well. Across the hall from her grandson's room, another child, this one five years old, was suffering in silence.

"Yes," I said nodding.

"I know you're not supposed to talk about other patients," she said with a halt to her voice. "But I've seen the news reports about an abused boy and can't help but notice the detectives coming from that room." She paused, then added, "The news said she did it because her son wouldn't clean his room."

I broke her gaze without responding, the new confidentiality laws very much on my mind.

I wondered who had heard the screams of that child as his mother beat him with a coat hanger? Whose spiritual radar had been tuned in to the pain that must have swelled in that home until things exploded? During the past twenty-four hours the staff had done everything they could to revive the cries of this child. The doctor pushed on his pressure points, watching for some signs of wincing. The nurses tapped his reflex points, praying for some sort of jerking. The surgeon shined her bright light into his eyes, looking for some sign of flinching.

Nothing. No groans. No cries. No screams.

"Chaplain!" the grandmother's anguished voice rose a notch.

"Yes?" I answered, feeling like screaming myself.

"He's only five! How could anyone do that?"

I looked down.

"I know you can't answer that," she said with some understanding.

Then, looking toward her grandson's room, the grandmother simply said, "I think mine's stopped screaming now. Do you think you might come in and say a prayer?"

"Sure."

There were too many things that afternoon I had no answer for, but as I prayed, the words of the psalmist came to mind: "Hear my prayer, O LORD, listen to my cry for help; be not deaf to my weeping" (Psalm 39:12).

EVIDENCE OF THINGS HOPED FOR

"Your staff seemed a bit chatty this afternoon," I told Wendy, the assistant nurse manager in the NICU.

"Oh, what seemed to be on their mind?" Wendy asked.

"Hope," I declared.

"Well, Chaplain, hope's a good thing, right?" she asked, puzzled at my look of concern. "I'm hoping so," I said, risking a bad pun to fill a difficult moment. "But if you have a minute, I'd like to say more."

Wendy shoved a chair in my direction.

"It's about our ECMO baby," I said. Pronounced EK-mo by the staffers, the acronym stands for extracorporeal membrane oxygenation, a therapy used to help babies suffering from severe heart and lung failure. ECMO essentially acts as a temporary heart/lung machine and gives the heart or lungs some rest so they can heal. It's used as a last resort when a baby isn't responding to conventional treatment.

In other words, we use ECMO when there isn't much hope. And when this baby arrived on our unit three days earlier, no one was feeling very hopeful. She'd been transferred from a hospital across the state where she'd first been admitted due to an infection that was quickly robbing her heart of any chance of sustaining life. With two nurses in tow, she had come into our NICU, where a sterile field was quickly readied. In moments, the staff inserted tubes into her neck so the machine could pump the blood from her body and oxygenate it in place of her poorly performing lungs.

While the procedure was being done, I sat with the parents outside the NICU. The mother's shoulders heaved in reaction to the unspeakable news. The healthy baby the parents had brought home only a month prior was now the subject of a doctors' discussion about the possibility of a heart transplant.

During the next three days, pediatric and neonatal nurses worked feverishly, attending to the baby's every need. The nurses worked double shifts, communicated closely with the doctors about each minor adjustment, and never blinked.

Now, as the assistant nurse manager and I sat talking, hope was seeping into the neonatal unit, and the nurses were wondering aloud whether they should be nurturing it or suppressing it. They couldn't help but show "cautious optimism" as the echocardiograms indicated steady improvement. They were struggling with their feelings, wondering, *Dare we hope?* And even, *What should we hope for?*

Sometimes we can only hope that our patients and their families will find the resources they need to make it through a tragedy. Sometimes we hope the difficulty will not be a long one that demands every resource they have: financial, social, and spiritual.

The truth is that what we hope for is most often tied to the kind of faith we have. But does hoping for anything less than a perfect outcome reflect a lack of faith?

Writing to a group of Jews who had lost hope because of the Roman occupation, the unknown author of the book of Hebrews suggested that hope had such a close relationship to faith that faith was literally "the substance of things hoped for, the evidence of things not seen" (11:1 KJV).

For a week, this baby was beset with a deep and unseen infection. The visual "evidence" did not indicate a good outcome. Yet for several days, parents and nurses prayed and hoped for an outcome that seemed contrary to that medical evidence. Eventually, as the tests began to indicate improvement, the staff and parents saw the "substance" of the things they had hoped for, the "evidence of things not seen." In a few days, that evidence prompted the doctors to remove the baby girl from all external support and return a healing child to the arms of her parents.

EIGHTY MINUTES OF PARENTING

Despite popular belief, Disney does not have a corner on the title *The Happiest Place on Earth*. That distinction usually belongs to the labor and delivery department at your local hospital.

Usually.

But on the morning I met Sue Reed and her husband, Mike, I already knew it was not going to be a usual day.

Sue and Mike married in their early forties. Blessed with one healthy child, Samantha, they were inspired to try for another. After a few difficult starts, Sue turned up pregnant in May 2003, two months shy of her forty-fourth birthday. They named their expected baby Gabriella Grace—GiGi for short.

Because babies born to older mothers tend to carry a greater risk of genetic deformities, Sue's doctors scheduled her for immediate genetic testing. A week after the test, Sue awoke with a feeling that *something's not OK*. Later that afternoon, a doctor's call confirmed her suspicion. The doctor told Sue that GiGi had trisomy 18, which meant she had an extra eighteenth chromosome.

Sue said, recalling that phone call, "I struggled to hear more, even as I began shutting down."

The "more" she was hearing was the doctor telling her that most women opt to terminate these pregnancies. While Mike and Sue spent the weekend "asking the hard question of what God was doing here," Sue couldn't help but recall a previous abortion she had had in her youth, a procedure "that punctured my heart forever," she said.

"I knew I couldn't do it again. I knew in my heart of hearts that God made GiGi exactly the way she was supposed to be made. I know that Scripture says, 'Before I formed you in the womb I knew you, before you were born I set you apart' (Jeremiah 1:5).

"God was asking me to honor this life," she said. "She was our daughter with a bad diagnosis, but that was secondary. Nevertheless, that diagnosis was like an end to my pregnancy. At each doctor's visit, I was sure that this time GiGi wouldn't have a heartbeat."

But GiGi's heart continued to beat, and the doctors began anticipating her live birth. They asked Sue how she wanted to care for GiGi after she was born. Sue remembers the doctor asking, with tears in her eyes, "How do you want this to play out?"

Sue and Mike instructed the doctor not to resuscitate but instead to offer all comfort care possible. "We just want to meet her and love her, to hold her and be with her. We want to know and love our daughter as long as she's with us," Sue said.

The night before the birth, Sue wrote a letter to GiGi in which she explained that "some people only dream of angels, but I get to actually give birth to one and then hold her in my arms. I am so very blessed. See you tomorrow, sweet girl."

On February 5, 2004, at 10:00 a.m., I entered the labor and delivery department to meet a couple who looked like any other expectant parents. They carried a video camera. They knew, however, that their camera would record the two most sacred moments of life—birth and death—all on one tape. Twenty minutes after Mike and I dressed in surgical scrubs, GiGi emerged, looking perfect.

"I expected a deformed baby," Sue admitted, "but she was beautiful. She was like a visitor from heaven. It was like God showing us that what we did was right, to honor this little life all the way to the end in spite of her impending fatality. Every life is precious, no matter how short. It should be God's decision when to call us home, not mine, or a doctor's, or even society's. God's timing is always perfect. I remember my heart exploding with joy that I had truly experienced God's perfect, divine will being done, that I had been obedient to it, and that GiGi never suffered but was just held and kissed by Michael and me until she died in Michael's arms. We knew that she knew we loved her, wanted her, and were there for her until she returned home."

GiGi lived just a little longer than an hour.

"It struck home with me that God hears, sees, and answers prayers," Sue said. "Even though I'd wished for a better outcome, I'm grateful God chose us. I never thought I could walk through something like this. It's made me realize how every moment in life is important—even if it's just eighty minutes. I packed a lot of parenthood into those eighty minutes."

Later Sue added, "Ever since this happened, I think about 'the moment.' GiGi's life was that moment. Sometimes love is for a moment. Sometimes it's for a lifetime. And sometimes a lifetime is a moment."

Learn more about trisomy 18 at
www.trisomy18support.org and see GiGi's Web site at
http://homepage.mac.com/reedsync/blogwavestudio/index.html.

THE PRAYERS OF BEGINNING

Braids of human hair hanging on the sanctuary walls at the Church of San Juan Barrio in Cotija de la Paz, Mexico, silently testified to the sacrificial prayers of the women who came there seeking desperate miracles. Inchi Sugarman was one of them.

After losing three children to miscarriages, Inchi went there on a pilgrimage seeking the holiest of all things—newborn life. Kneeling at the tomb of the venerated Mama Maurita, she prayed for the gift of just one more child, her fifth. It was a prayer she might not have prayed had she realized it would cost her every drop of blood throbbing through her hopeful chest.

Yet when I met the family one year later in their California home, Inchi and her husband, Barry, responded gratefully to the answered prayer by vowing to name their child Maura Rose— they would call her "Maurita"—after the woman entombed outside the little Mexican church.

No one would have expected the circuitous route the prayer's answer would take. Inchi spent the first three months bleeding, and tests seemed to question the miracle, showing that the unborn Maurita wasn't getting critical nutrition. Complicating things even more, Inchi soon developed gestational diabetes. Her doctors sent her to bed, ordering her to eat and sleep as much as possible. Nevertheless, each additional test introduced more questions and pointed more certainly toward delivering the baby through a C-section.

The surgery was planned for her eighth month, but on the night prior to the scheduled delivery, Inchi's bleeding restarted, and doctors ordered her into the operating room. Inchi greeted one of the nurses there with a foreboding prediction, telling her she had a "bad feeling about all of this." She handed the caring nurse holy water and asked her to use it if something went wrong.

"I could tell Inchi was nervous and fearful," said Barry. "But her thoughts were only for Maurita."

She had no inkling that the holy water might be used on her own behalf.

Despite Inchi's worries, the doctors' work proceeded routinely, and at 1:29 a.m., Saturday, October 4, 2003, doctors pulled the four-pound, one-ounce Maurita into the world, pink and healthy.

Barry brought Maurita to her mother, and Inchi managed a faint smile then said weakly, "I'm just so tired."

"At that point," Barry said, "Inchi lifted her head off the table and made a loud, gurgling scream."

Suddenly all the wrong buzzers started buzzing, and Barry and Maurita were quickly ushered from the room. Seconds later, Barry heard the ominous call: "Code blue. Any cardiologist to labor and delivery, stat!"

Scores of people came rushing from all directions, and Inchi was hurriedly returned to the operating room. Barry sat rocking in a chair outside the OR, praying and making difficult phone calls to give family members moment-to-moment information. Inside the OR, doctors worked on one side of Inchi pumping in units of blood and on the other side trying to stop the bleeding.

A few hours later, she was wheeled into the ICU, her condition still very uncertain.

Saturday was a day of desperation. A priest was called to administer last rites, and neonatal nurses laid Maurita on her mother's chest, perhaps for the last time. Emergency airline tickets were secured for family members after an ICU nurse tersely ordered Barry to "get them here, now!"

Yet just a few hours later, Inchi miraculously began to awaken. Lucid enough to be writing notes through the myriad of drugs and the discomfort of a breathing tube down her throat, she also began asking the staff about what had happened.

As the sun rose Sunday morning, Barry did the only thing he knew to do: he took his family to early mass. "The Scripture reading was about marriage," he recalled, "and that was as close as I came to losing it."

When Barry returned to the hospital after mass, the doctors told him he should expect Inchi to require several weeks of recovery, but two hours later, the agitated Inchi seemed to be favoring other plans. Surprised at her feistiness, the doctors decided to remove her breathing tube. She not only breathed on her own, but thirty-six hours after delivery, she was sitting on the edge of her bed eating solid food and talking about the upcoming election in which Arnold Schwarzenegger was running for governor.

"I told you I should have done an absentee ballot," she scolded her husband.

But the talk was of more than elections. Barry narrated the frightening events that had brought Inchi to the ICU. Through the ordeal, Inchi had gained thirty pounds in fluid and "bled out every drop of her own blood," reported Barry.

Over the next week, Inchi came to understand that she had experienced a rare and deadly form of birth complication—an amniotic fluid embolism. Her survival had hinged on the split-second reaction of our medical staff.

Most of the time, a mother afflicted with AFE dies.

"When I was in the OR," Inchi later reported, "I was aware that something was going on, but I couldn't get up or see anything. I was in total darkness with twenty different voices talking at once. There was nothing I could do except pray. I prayed until I wasn't conscious anymore. When I woke up, I didn't understand why I hadn't died. There had to be a reason. I'm not sure whether I know now. I feel like my life isn't my own. It isn't just for me to live. It's for me to do something for God," she said.

"When Inchi began to ask me why this happened," Barry said, "my first reaction was that it could have happened to many different women and they would have attributed the recovery to any number of things—luck or science. But Inchi has a unique spiritual focus. To be able to talk about this as a miracle is a way that helps introduce others to faith.

"There is no question in our minds that this was a first-class miracle, but God effects miracles in many different ways," Barry said. "And the way God effected this miracle is that absolutely everybody did everything they were supposed to do at the moment they were supposed to do it."

THE GIFT

Laurel was born such a perfect baby that Elizabeth and Dave Gates considered her a gift. Born January 16, 2002, the third of three girls, baby Laurel came home from the hospital on Elizabeth's birthday. Smiling when she was only a few days old and sprouting curly blonde hair in the first few months, Laurel was the kind of kid people stop and fuss over while Christmas shopping at the mall.

With such a perfect beginning, it seemed quite odd, a few months later, for Laurel's great-aunt to mysteriously proclaim from her deathbed, "Tell Elizabeth her baby will be all right!" At the time, no one could know Laurel faced any danger. But in the winter of 2004, the meaning of her great-aunt's words were revealed when Elizabeth returned to her childhood home in Modesto, California, bringing potted plants to help her children celebrate her grandmother's seventy-fifth birthday.

After a waffle breakfast, the family adjourned to the front yard, where the adults worked at transplanting the potted plants while Laurel and her sisters played nearby, running in and out of the house. "My last recollection of Laurel," said Elizabeth, "was when I called her back from the end of the driveway; she'd wandered too close to the street. I told her, 'Good job, you came back!'"

But as quickly as Elizabeth returned to her plants, Laurel was gone again. The second disappearance prompted Elizabeth to begin asking those questions no preschooler's parent likes to ask.

"Who's seen Laurel? We need to find her," Elizabeth said. The search escalated quickly into some dramatic mental pictures. "I thought, *She may be dead.* I know that's dramatic, but after a few minutes, that's what I'd already begun thinking. I ran through the house and into the backyard, where I suddenly remembered the backyard pond."

Elizabeth's eyes shot toward the pond, and there she saw something "my mind wasn't letting me see," she said. She wanted it to be a giant lily pad or a discarded bucket, but it wasn't.

It was Laurel, floating facedown in the water.

Elizabeth remembers "grabbing Laurel by the back of her pants, but she was completely limp, like a cold fish. Her eyes were rolled back slightly, and her tongue hung out of her mouth. I started screaming, 'Oh my God, she's already gone!'"

As she had done earlier when Laurel had strayed too close to the end of the driveway, Elizabeth urged her daughter, "Laurel, come back! Come back!"

She laid Laurel down to start CPR, and water began to drain from the little girl. As Elizabeth started the CPR she recalled from a class she'd taken nine years earlier, Laurel's grandmother called 911.

Following the ambulance to the hospital, Elizabeth frantically called her airline pilot husband, Dave, sobbing out the words, "I'm so sorry! I'm so sorry!"

It would take him hours to get there, but he began that long trip by first assuring his wife of his love for her and their children.

Once in the ER, Elizabeth waited with her family, anxiously watching the door and anticipating the worst news. In a few minutes she was told that Laurel had a faint pulse and needed to be transferred to another hospital—the one where I work, Sutter Medical Center in Sacramento. Before the transfer, the family was invited to visit Laurel.

"She had a body temperature of eighty-eight degrees," Elizabeth said. "I bent down to whisper that I loved her and I was so very sorry. I sung her favorite lullaby. And I heard the nurses comment on her ominous twitching."

One by one the relatives came in, and the family's priest came to pray. His prayer acknowledged that the God who created Laurel could recreate her. He prayed that she would be whole and new, as she was intended to be.

"At that point, I felt really connected with God, and for the first time, I knew I had to pray that Laurel would completely recover," Elizabeth said.

After Laurel's transfer to Sutter, she met Dr. David Smith, whom she described later as "kind, but brutally honest."

"I wish I could tell you everything will be all right," Dr. Smith said, "but I can't. She's taken a great insult." And then, holding his index finger slightly above his thumb, he said, "There's a hair of hope, but that's hope. The first twenty-four hours are critical." He paused a moment before saying something else. Something that made Liz gasp for breath. "Then we'll look at what remains of her brain functions," he told her.

After receiving that news, the family joined hands as Liz offered her prayer, telling God how grateful she was to have Laurel. She promised that if God would do a miracle and make her child as new as the morning, "I won't waste the miracle. I'll declare your awesome, beautiful, and loving mercy to anyone who will hear it."

Elizabeth's sister shared a prayer as well, along with the words of Psalm 34:7: "The angel of the LORD encamps around those who fear him, and he delivers them."

Elizabeth worked to memorize the verse. "I repeated it throughout the night in my heart," she said. "The next morning, when the doctors came in with their first report, I remember feeling as if the sun was coming out of the dark sky."

Doctors told the family that the refrigerated blanket Laurel was sleeping on could be turned off, and she also would be weaned off the medication as they watched for some level of activity. But as Laurel left the bounds of the medication, she showed no signs of responding to any type of stimulus. Elizabeth remembers the neurologist giving her that *I'm so sorry* look. But she disregarded it and knelt beside Laurel to sing:

> *Hush, little baby, don't say a word,*
> *Mama's going to show you a hummingbird.*
> *And if that hummingbird should fly,*
> *Mama's going to show you the evening sky.*

Miraculously, as every eye in the room flooded with tears, Laurel opened her eyes. Yet even as surprised expressions overcame the staff, the doctors cautioned that it might be no more than a reflex action.

The positive signs continued. Dave had arrived during the night, and as Liz stood outside the room later that morning, he came running out of Laurel's room to tell her, "She's waking up, Liz! She's waking up!"

Elizabeth scrambled to her daughter's bedside. When Laurel saw her mother, she puckered her lips and said hoarsely, "I love you." They were the very words Elizabeth had asked God to let her hear from Laurel again. Then, turning to Dave, Laurel called, "Dada," and when Dave leaned toward her, she kissed him.

Throughout the afternoon, as Laurel showed her recognition of everyone, the family members—and the doctors—fought back tears of astonishment. "We're declaring that God had a hand in this!" Elizabeth told me.

Dr. Dan Falco, the intensive-care specialist (a physician called an *intensivist*) told the family that none of this could be explained in medical terms. The "laboratory results weren't compatible with a good outcome," he said.

Over the next few days, Laurel fought an uphill battle as she labored to breathe, but, "Ultimately God had every bit to do with her healing," Elizabeth told me. "Some people thought the cold pond had worked in her favor, and perhaps that helped a bit. But the doctors all thought the pond couldn't have been near cold enough."

"The water temperature really shouldn't have made any difference at all," said Dr. Falco, whose own faith was tremendously affirmed. "God did this one, and it may well be the defining point of Laurel's life."

Elizabeth remained at her daughter's bedside for six days;

she spent hours staring into Laurel's eyes. "Children don't usually let you gaze very long, but Laurel let me look until I could see into her soul. I kept thanking her for coming back."

Months after the near drowning, Elizabeth reported that Laurel is "doing wonderfully. She's learning new words and has a deeper joy now when she's having fun."

Elizabeth admits that she doesn't really know "why it all happened, but I do know that God works through angels, doctors, nurses, and saints. I believe, but it will always be a mystery that I'll never understand."

It's a mystery the apostle Paul compared to looking in a dim mirror: "Now we see but a poor reflection as in a mirror; then we shall see face to face. Now I know in part; then I shall know fully, even as I am fully known. And now these three remain: faith, hope and love. But the greatest of these is love" (1 Corinthians 13:12–13).

"WHERE IS MY CHILD?"

One day, in the midst of a passionate hunt for fried chicken, I gave a chaplain friend some advice: "Never, never, never," I advised the new chaplain, "give a patient your personal phone number."

"But," he asked, "what if you like the person so much you could adopt their kids?"

"Well, then, I'd say that fits under the category of . . . never!" I insisted.

Despite my strong pronouncement, I had broken my own rule too often in the last few months; my emotional edict was my own way of resolving to do better. Suddenly the ringing of my cell phone caused me to miss the exit for chicken.

"Hello."

Sobs swelled through the phone like ocean waves threatening to drown both swimmer and rescuer. "Chaplain, where is he? I mean . . . , Eric's in heaven, right?" The voice belonged to the mother of a special child who had recently died in our pediatric intensive care unit.

"Yes, I feel certain he is," I said, shifting gears from fast food to food for thought.

"What's going on for you right now, Sarah?"

"I'm having nightmares; I dream that Eric is smothering and can't breathe." More sobs. "I need a favor," she said. "I liked what you wrote about Eric. Will you write something for me again?"

"Like what?"

"Could you write something that would remind me where Eric is and what it was like for him after he died? Tell me what he's feeling."

The Bible contains many references to heaven, but Sarah wasn't looking for biblical authority. She was looking to share in another parent's deepest hope. Living these past months in pain that was raw and brutal, she was trying to make it through her personal hell on earth—one day at a time, one prayer at a time, one phone call at a time.

So I gave it a try, and told her my dream of heaven.

"Sarah, I don't know for sure what heaven's like. The Bible tells me God prepares it as a 'place not made with hands'—so it's probably more than we could ever imagine. And if it's made by God, then heaven must be made of the best of us, of who we are, of all our hearts can collectively imagine."

Sarah was quiet on the other end of the line and, as she soaked up what I had said, I sensed maybe she needed more. Truth is, I needed more too.

"Sarah, you cared for Eric every hour of every day for years. Your love formed a cocoon of heaven for him right here on earth. God has done no less for Eric in that he created a heaven designed by a mother's love and a father's care," I said. "When I think of Eric in heaven, I see him in a place where his lungs are filled with the freshest air from the most pristine mountain peaks. It's a place where he doesn't need to struggle to find his legs. He can walk and run and jump. He can dance with butterflies and sing with angels.

"He can talk and hear and understand. He knows the joy of a million rainbow waterfalls. He knows a Father who loves him, and he is filled with the memory of a mother's lullaby to comfort him."

Sarah and I spoke a little longer, and when we ended our conversation, I resolved to amend my advice to the other chaplain. I let him know that sometimes God knows who needs to talk to us. I think God knew I needed to talk to Sarah as much as she needed to talk to me, so he gave her the number—via my own big mouth. God does, indeed, work in mysterious ways. So my new policy is, "Never, never, never give a patient your personal phone number—unless it's God's idea."

DEAR ADRIANA, . . .

Recently the mother of a cancer patient shared with me some thoughts about her daughter's treatment. Together we worked to put those thoughts into this letter to her daughter.

Dear Adriana,

It seems like only yesterday that I sat watching you accept your sixth-grade diploma. My eyes clouded with proud tears as I simultaneously mourned the passing of slipping years. One moment I was kissing your "owies" and playing patty-

cake with you—the next moment you were plunging into womanhood.

I know it's a little selfish, but I wanted you to be my little girl forever. I wanted to worry and hover over the busyness of your childhood. It may sound silly, but I was looking forward to worrying with you about junior high boys and staying up late with you to work on algebra and eat ice cream.

Who could have imagined that my nights would be filled with a haunting worry of how you'd survive cancer treatments? Who could have imagined that I'd watch my little girl suffer a hell that no child should endure?

Never did I want to imagine that I'd be holding your soul in my arms as you mourned the loss of your hair and watched your dreams disappear into the blackest of midnights known as chemotherapy and radiation.

Never did I dare imagine that you'd spend every third week of forty weeks ingesting the poison of chemo, flushing your lines, taking untold shots, and swallowing eighty pills a day. Never did I imagine that you'd outline this torture with the grace of a woman and the innocent heart of a child—only to be born again out of your pain.

Never could I know that you'd approach this treacherous journey with unimaginable bravery, doing all you could to shield us from your fear and pain. But even as you continued your brave march, I could see in your well-worn face that you wanted nothing more than to win this fight and come home. Yet you should know that even brave people get weary.

Never did I imagine knowing a day when my teenage daughter's biggest dream would not be for material things but to take regular showers and blow-dry her newly grown hair. The *fact that you have just one more treatment to complete gives me the most indescribable joy I've known since the cold shudder of fear first shattered our world last year.*

The journey has been unimaginable, but now I'm finally allowing myself to imagine the most beautiful light at the end of our tunnel. And it's light that finds you center stage. It's light that shines on a wonderfully regular kid who is playing video games, going to school, and yes, even finding some joy in homework.

No one will ever imagine how happy I'll be to see you complete this amazing journey and hear that your final test in two weeks will declare you cancer free. Yet I know there is no guarantee, so I pray with everything I am that you'll never repeat this torture. I hold in my heart a prayer that you'll walk through life appreciating the gifts bestowed upon you.

Adriana, we've been so fortunate to have friends who have been our guiding light, our hope when we felt there was none, our angels, and even the hands of God. We never could have lived through this year without their love and prayers. You are proof to me that the world really is a good place and there really are wonderful people whose giving comes straight from their heart.

With much love,
Your mother and best friend.

Then Adriana's mom asked me for something else. "Being the greedy gal I am," she said, "I'm going to ask for one last prayer for Adriana. We've been told that she will never be out of the woods until she's been cancer free for over five years. Please pray that the tests continue to find her to be in perfect health and that she flies through these next five years without a trace of cancer. That is my fondest prayer."

And it's my prayer too.

ONE MORE BREATH

Sometimes I have days that begin so well I describe them as Mary Poppins so often did: "practically perfect in every way."

One such "practically perfect" day began when my teenage son was actually ready for school on time—and without giving me any lip. The gesture created a perfect snowball effect, for his punctuality meant we left on time. Leaving on time meant that after I dropped him off I had the perfect commute without a single traffic delay. No delay meant getting the perfect shaded parking spot. Then, to top it all off, as I walked from the parking lot, I found the green-vested crossing guard in the crosswalk beckoning me safely into the hospital. Overwhelmed with such perfect synchronicity, my head filled with the syrupy lyrics of "Singin' in the Rain," even though the day was so perfect there wasn't a cloud in the sky.

When my day starts out this perfect, I like to reward myself with a cup of hot chocolate. Sure enough, the perfect cup was served with a greeting as sweet as the chocolate itself: "Chaplain, is that a new tie? Very cool!"

On the go with the chocolate, I found an elevator waiting to shuttle me nonstop to my third-floor office, where I found that my co-worker had already unlocked the doors and booted up our computer. After reading e-mails from two appreciative readers (whose taste in newspaper columnists seemed perfect), I headed to the pediatric floor for a visit with my five-year-old friend Opal.

Dressed in street clothes, Opal was awaiting discharge orders and greeted me with the largest smile ever pasted on such a small face. "Swing me! Swing me!" she said, seizing my fingers with a full-handed grip. As we swung, I caught a glimpse of two nurses giving us one of those *aren't they perfectly cute!* smiles. In a few moments, Opal's doctor arrived, and I said my good-byes to pediatrics and wandered off toward the pediatric intensive care unit (which, you've probably guessed by now, we pronounce "pick-u"), musing, *Why can't every day be as perfect as this one?*

But in the PICU, my perfect day took on a new perspective. I met a thirteen-year-old boy named Alex, whose parents had learned on a not-so-perfect Mother's Day that their son's cancer had returned. As I visited with Alex's mother outside his room, an alarm suddenly called her back to his bedside. I followed. As she glanced at the blood-oxygen indicator and noticed the levels falling dangerously low, she expressed an urgent motherly command: "Breathe, Alex. Just breathe. Take a deep breath."

As she watched her son's chest rise and fall a few times, the indicator showed Alex's blood oxygen returning to normal levels. But this mom wasn't taking anything for granted.

"Take one more," she urged through a deep inhale she hoped he would mimic. Then, placing an approving hand on Alex's forehead, she said, "There, that's perfect. Just perfect."

Suddenly the syrupy "Singin' in the Rain" lyrics vanished from my head and were replaced with a new song: "Holy, Holy, Holy." I knew I was standing in the presence of perfect and holy love, an experience that instantly redefined my understanding of a perfect day.

Who was I kidding? There was nothing in my life that had me singing in the rain. There *was* no rain in my life, only sunshine, with not even a slow elevator to mar my morning. Yet here was a family in a downpour of anguish, huddled together and trying to keep each other warm, their hearts full of so much love it transformed all who witnessed it.

It humbled me to be a part of it, to be in the presence of such holy love. Now I know that a perfect day needn't be defined by events that happen or don't happen. Nope. "Perfect" is about knowing the kind of love this young man knew, love that was there for him, no matter what, to help him in the most basic things, to love him through the best and the worst parts of his life.

May we all be blessed to share such perfectly holy love.

BURDENS TOO GREAT

I confess there is a small, sadistic streak in me that revels in the embarrassment of people who suddenly realize a chaplain has heard their off-color remarks. They look at me as though they are suddenly seven years old again and I've become their mother, threatening to wash out their mouth with a bar of soap.

"Jeez, Chaplain, I'm sorry," they say. "I didn't see you standing there."

I'm not a grammar expert, but in moments like these I jokingly step into the role of theological grammarian. For instance, if you pronounce God's last name as "Damn," I might say, "No, no, no. He hasn't used that name since Sodom and Gomorrah."

If you respond to frustration by saying, "Oh, God," I'll attempt to throw my voice into a deep baritone and say, "Yes, my son?" If you blurt out, "Jesus!" when something goes wrong, I might ask, "Was that a prayer?" If I sneeze, and you respond with "God bless you," I'll say, "Thank you. He does." Or, if I feel devilish, I might say, "Thank you. She does."

Chaplains hear it all, and if we respond at all to such accidental slurs and misstatements, most of us do so jokingly. But there is one statement I'm quick to correct whenever I hear it. If I hear someone try to explain another's tragedy with the words, "God won't give you more than you can handle," I can't help myself. I'll blurt out, "The Bible doesn't say that!" and hurry to set the facts straight.

The quote is a poor paraphrase of 1 Corinthians 10:13, which is translated in the New International Version as, "He will not let you be tempted beyond what you can bear. But when you are tempted, he will also provide a way out so that you can stand up under it." The folksy paraphrase of the verse burdens people with an understanding that God "gives" us calamities.

I guess I had heard that misquote one too many times on the afternoon when I stumbled into a woman in the oncology ward who was losing her son to AIDS. She seemed to have that misstatement wrapped around her neck, and she was burdened by its weight. I didn't sense that she had any kind of superhuman strength, so it didn't seem reasonable to conclude that God required this woman to have the strength of the Greek god Atlas and, all by herself, hold up her world.

"Chaplain, can you talk with my son?" she asked the moment she met me.

"Sure."

"He has AIDS, and you might have to put on some protective clothing," she instructed.

AIDS protocol did not require the clothing, but I quickly learned that her son had more than AIDS. He also had hepatitis B and tuberculosis, and as if that weren't enough, his room was "hot" with the radioactive isotopes used to treat his cancer. His projectile vomiting was a serious danger to staff, and that was just the danger he posed to *us*. He was also in reverse isolation, which meant that healthy people posed a big risk to him. His immune system was shot, and a sneeze by any of us might finish him off. So I entered the room looking like the Sta-Puft marshmallow man, "double-wrapped for freshness" inside a space suit.

The young man sincerely expressed how glad he was to see me—with no shortage of expletives. But I definitely sensed this was not the time to play theological grammarian. He had played a dangerous game with his life, combining illicit drugs and both male and female prostitutes, all washed down with a considerable amount of alcohol. The results had left him devastatingly ill—and somewhat delusional. Now he knew he was dying, and he was sorry for the pain he had caused his mother.

After I finished my visit, I found her talking to the social workers outside her son's room. She told us she had once been the Sunday school director of her church, but now, people in the church rarely spoke to her. Then she quoted it—that misstatement I dreaded: "People tell me God won't give me more than I can handle, but I don't know . . . ," she said, her voice breaking. "Having both sons die of AIDS is more than I can bear."

It takes a lot to give experienced hospital professionals a cold chill, but one went down the spine of everyone listening to that grief-stricken mom. *Had she said* two *sons?* That would mean this patient was not her *only* son; he was her only *living* son. And she had been so heavily burdened with this misquote of Scripture that she now had the added burden of believing she was failing a test sent from God.

Jesus jumped all over the preachers of his day for burdening people with loads they would not—could not—carry themselves. That's another reason I find this to be one of the most reckless misquotes of Scripture; God doesn't give us our share of calamities. Much of what we are "given" is either given to us by others or self-acquired. I assured this distraught mother that while this ordeal seemed to be much more than any human being could possibly handle, it was also something God himself may have struggled to endure as he watched the death of his only Son. The Bible says the sky darkened over Calvary, at least for a time, and I've often wondered if that darkness was a sign that watching his Son die was a bit more than even God could handle.

This devoted mother had already watched one son die, and now she was standing by helplessly as another son prepared for death. The difference between God's loss and hers was that, because of the way Jesus lived, there was still a miracle to offer this woman. It was the miracle of God's presence.

There was no way to make her situation better. There was no way to create a happy ending to our conversation and no point pretending otherwise. I simply held her hand and let her know that for the next several days, I would be there, along with several others. And together with God, we would help her shoulder this enormous burden.

DO YOU SEE WHAT I SEE?

"I had a crazy dream last night," I told my wife as I studied my daughter's senior portraits. "I dreamed our daughter [the one who has sported a butterfly tattoo since becoming of legal age last month] shaved her head."

Worried the dream might inspire more coming-of-age behavior, my wife begged, "Please don't tell her about that dream!"

Dreams can be funny. Some people think they can *reveal* reality while others see ways they can *forge* reality. And sometimes—as Pastor Randy Phillips of Creekside Covenant Church in Redmond, Washington, experienced last year—it's hard to tell which comes first, the dream or the reality. Phillips's church hosted a worship service to celebrate the rescue of a missing Redmond girl, Laura Hatch, seventeen. Sha Nohr came to that service to share the dream she'd had, a dream that led to Laura's rescue.

Laura was on her way home from a party on October 2, 2004, when her car left the road and careened into a ravine. She remained trapped there for eight days until a dream inspired Sha Nohr, the mother of Laura's friend, to search the area where she found Laura. Rescue crews were summoned, and as they worked to pull the dehydrated teenager from her car, Laura's parents were called to the site. There, according to Pastor Phillips, Sha Nor met Todd Hatch (Laura's dad) for the first time.

Since Laura was found, there has been an intense focus on Sha's remarkable dream, but in talking with the Hatch family's pastor, I found him a bit concerned that folks will hear the story and miss the real miracle. It's not the dream. It's "the miracle of people loving and helping each other," he said. "To see a family stretched, to hear neighbors offer them 'anything you need,' to watch people bring meals—so many that the family commented that one more casserole would leave them no place to live, to watch the friends of this remarkable young woman organize two hundred volunteers and lead a professional search party—this was the real miracle."

In a day when the news is full of stories on the workings of the global economy, this pastor saw a story about spiritual economy at work. "There's nothing wasted in God's economy," he said. "I've been getting e-mail from all over the planet. People say that, for whatever reason, they stopped and prayed for Laura. There is an intricacy in how God works. He works in spectacular ways."

The pastor admitted, "It was emotionally overwhelming. We felt sorrow for the possibilities that could have been considered. We went a whole week, and we were worried and scared, but the real story is that God has hope, and that hope is sustainable. When we begin to falter, God picks us up and says, 'I've got enough for all of us.'

"The family has a couple of requests," the pastor confided. "They ask that people continue to pray for Laura. And," he added, "let's pray for all our missing teenagers. Here in King County," he said, "eight hundred teenagers are missing. Second, the family wants to make sure that people hear their gratitude to God for every moment of this experience. They want people to hear the generosity of their community."

Pastor Phillips said he didn't fully understand how Nohr had been blessed with her rescue dream, but he was beginning to see how the workings of people coming together may have inspired it. "True, the dream is a remarkable element, but what God has done here is to give us a wonderful object lesson. The lesson is that this is what God's heart is like—reconciling people to him! And God did this visually with this sweetheart named Laura. That's the heartbeat of the story!" he exclaimed.

Perhaps the pastor summarized it best in this verse quoted from *The Message*: "If people can't see what God is doing, they stumble all over themselves; but when they attend to what he reveals, they are most blessed" (Proverbs 29:18).

ALICIA'S FEET . . . AND HER FATHER'S HANDS

Recently I've been struggling with some back pain. No, it's not from having three teenage children—at least not all of it. Some of it's from, well, from getting older. The pain's enough to make me wish I had a button to push and make it all go away.

Actually, there is such a button. It's called a PCA (patient-controlled analgesia) pump, and it's used in most hospitals. Each time the patient presses the button, a prescribed dose of pain medication is delivered intravenously, accompanied by a *ping*. The pump won't allow overdoses, so if the button is pressed before it's time for another dose, the apparatus remains silent and no medicine is delivered.

PCAs often are used in the pediatric cancer unit of our hospital. And never have I thought of those PCA pumps more vividly than I did on a routine visit with eighteen-year-old patient Alicia Kobrock.

Alicia was a ballerina battling cancer. During her teen years, the emotional music that kept her heart singing and her toes pointing consisted of family, faith, and dance. But in August 2002, Alicia's music modulated into a minor key when she was diagnosed with a high-grade cancerous sarcoma. Doctors urged an immediate and aggressive course of surgery, chemotherapy, and radiation.

The cancer responded quickly to treatment, but the toll of the yearlong regimen kept her sick at home during her sophomore high school year. In fall 2003, after a year of homeschooling, she returned to public school, where she enrolled in a photography class. The teacher challenged Alicia's artistic spirit by asking her students to take a photo of something "near and dear" to them. Alicia immediately thought of her ballet shoes.

"I thought of how hard I worked at dancing," explained Alicia. "I thought of what it meant to get my pointe shoes and how excited I was to be dancing, even though it hurt."

The hard-toed slippers, called pointe shoes or toe shoes, are especially designed and fitted for the dancer who is ready to move out of the soft slippers of beginning ballet.

Alicia's photograph of the three pairs of toe shoes she wore during her dancing career won first place in her age group's category in the 2004 California State Fair. In the photo, her first toe shoes are the ones showing the most wear. They bear the marks and scuffs from the falls and tumbles of a young dancer who had recently left the comfort and safety of flat shoes. Alicia's second pair of pointe shoes commemorate her successes at the height of her dancing. They seem to gleam with the confidence of someone bravely taking new risks. The third pair, the newest toe shoes, are almost unblemished; Alicia's days of dancing declined and then ended when her doctor diagnosed her cancer.

The cancer had eventually stabilized, giving her hope that she would dance again. But in February 2004, the malignancy grew, and the only dancing Alicia could do was on the stage of her memories.

During one particularly lucid visit with me, Alicia talked about the shoes. "Looking at them reminds me of the friends I danced with," she said. "We saw each other's mistakes, and it was OK. It was a time of fellowship with girls who shared something amazing. I loved the elegance of ballet. It was almost magic. Dance is how you feel, and being part of dancing is like being part of a song."

But as Alicia looked at the prize-winning photo, she admitted, "The pointe shoes were just a chapter of my life, and I've had to move on." Yet Alicia's accompanying poem about the shoes reveals just how important that chapter was:

Pointe in Time
My shoes tell the story of memories,
fun times, and ballet friends,
Ever dear to my heart,
Forever they will stay.
They were the shoes I was so proud to wear.
I danced in them and loved them.
They know my every step,
every fall, every thought,
and my joy and my pain.
They were my dreams and expression.
They called out my name.
Oh, how beauty and elegance flow
from their ribbons,
whispering old things.
As long as I love them
my memories will never fade.

During many of my visits, I knew that pain was consuming Alicia's body. On the most painful days, Alicia used her PCA to help ease the pain, and she looked to God for strength. "He is the One who has kept me going," she said. "We pray for healing, and until that healing comes, we will believe God is in control. He does amazing things. God is simply amazing!"

One day, as I walked through the doorway, I suddenly found my gaze fixed on her thumb, locked on the PCA button. Alicia was pressing it repeatedly, as if begging it to alleviate her pain.

But what she held in her other hand was far more hopeful. There I saw the hand of her father, Bob, and through that strong hand a miraculous and mighty strength streamed from father to daughter. Theirs was a grip of knowing and being known, a tender knowledge anchored deep in their hearts.

Still standing in the doorway, I couldn't stop my mind from fast-forwarding to a day I knew was coming—the day of Alicia's funeral. Oddly, I did not envision it as a memorial service but as a wedding—in particular, the part of the ceremony when the father of the bride traditionally pauses at the altar, unclasps his daughter's hand, kisses her, and escorts her into the arms of her beloved.

In the scene I imagined, Alicia gently turned loose of her earthly father's hand and stepped into the loving arms of the One she called her heavenly Father. And in that exchange, all pain ended forever and healing took place.

I don't remember a lot about our visit that afternoon, but I can tell you that Bob gripped Alicia's hand steadily for hours on end, and for endless days after that one.

Then, on March 20, 2005, in what the apostle Paul described as a "mystery," Alicia was transformed in the "twinkling of an eye," and Bob and Alicia's mother, Linda, entrusted their beautiful ballerina, with all her pain and her unrealized potential, into the hands of the One who would fill her with joy beyond anything imaginable.

Isaiah 52:7 says, "How beautiful . . . are the feet of the messenger bringing good news" (MSG). The good news that Alicia's lovely dancing feet bring us is the reminder that God dances with us through the best and the most difficult times of life. And yes, Alicia, God *is* "simply amazing!"

WITHOUT GRACE, IT'S A SMALL WORLD

The most difficult attraction for me at Disneyland has always been It's a Small World. I can't stand being trapped in that setting with all those tinny, squeaky little voices singing about their small world.

Nevertheless, I still choose to work in a small world—literally—when I head into the pediatric ward. The voices I hear there aren't confined to happy little voices, however. Sometimes I hear the voice of a mother bargaining for her child's life or a father promising to become the "man of God" he's supposed to be if God will heal his child.

But the voices don't always promise, beg, or bargain. Sometimes they're angry voices that vehemently deny God's existence while in the same breath curse the nonexistent God. I've heard these voices threaten lawsuits while choking out their sobbing prayers that beg for the end of their child's pain. I've even seen the hole where a father put his fist through a wall.

Yet as angry as they get, I often hear voices that ask forgiveness for the anger. "I've told God I'm sorry for getting angry at him," they tell me.

As I think about that type of angry bargaining, I find it helpful to compare how God handles that anger with the way I might handle the same anger from one of my children. I consider what might happen if I grounded one of my teenage daughters for coming home too late. Perhaps she'd apologize and then ask to borrow the car again. Perhaps I might respond to her apology by saying something like, "I'm sorry, but you're grounded. Maybe next week you can borrow the car again, but not this week."

But if, instead of apologizing, she responded to me by cursing at me and stomping off to her room, how would you expect me to respond the next morning when she barely manages a mumbled, "Sorry 'bout last night"?

A. Refuse her breakfast.
B. Tell her to start packing.
C. Ban her to eternal hellfire.
D. Kiss her, tell her I love her, and say, "Let's talk some more."

Although it might be tempting to ask, "Am I limited to just one answer?" I suspect most of us parents would select option D. That's because while parents aren't perfect we're created in God's image, and thus we can love and forgive our children when they make mistakes—just as God loves and forgives us. When we rant and rave at God from the depths of a hurting heart, he also chooses option D.

That's what grace is all about. We don't have to be afraid of making an irreparable mistake because God has promised to forgive us. I guess that's why I've always had a problem with people who adamantly insist that the rest of us are in one of two groups—those who are heaven bound and those who are toast. It's just not that cut and dried.

"Which of you, if his son asks for bread, will give him a stone?" Jesus asked. "Or if he asks for a fish, will give him a snake? If you, then, though you are evil, know how to give good gifts to your children, how much more will your Father in heaven give good gifts to those who ask him!" (Matthew 7:9–11).

The passage teaches that even no-good parents know how to give good things to their own children. And if that's true, then

God must be willing to give and forgive in ways unimaginable to our finite views.

Sometimes I think the church has made itself a kind of dispensary where God's love is something that's kept under lock and key, only to be dispensed through the right combination of confessions, creeds, and conditions. That's not the true picture. His love isn't a controlled item or a banned substance. It's unconditional.

Those folks who see God's love as having some kind of limit—who think, for instance, that he stops loving us when we get angry with him—will always be the ones who limit themselves to the crumbs of forgiveness falling from God's table. For them, I suppose it will always be "a small world after all . . . a small, small world."

AN UNUSUAL RING TO THE DAY

Personally, I don't have much use for toe rings. It's not that I dislike them; it's just that, until recently, I didn't see much value in them. But then I discovered a few purposes.

The first occasion came when I met a mother whose fourteen-year-old daughter was a cancer patient. The mother offered her daughter a costume-jewelry toe ring she'd bought in the hospital's gift shop, but her daughter declined, calling it "dorky."

I told the girl I thought it was pretty.

"If you think it's so pretty," she scoffed, "why don't *you* wear it?"

Toe Ring Lesson #1: never dispute the opinion of a sick teenager.

"OK," I said. "I will."

Hoping the mother or daughter would stop me, I began

removing my shoe. But to my dismay, no word of protest came from either of them. So my shoe came off, and then I removed my sock, which, considering how nauseated cancer patients can easily become, wasn't exactly a good career move. Nevertheless, I slid the ring onto my little toe and then put my sock and shoe back on. That's when the patient's pain medicine kicked in, and she started howling in laughter.

Toe Ring Lesson #2: helping a fourteen-year-old bald girl laugh through her cancer treatment is a good use of a toe ring.

Later that day, I had a doctor's appointment that caused me to formulate Toe Ring Lesson #3: don't let your doctor see you wearing a plastic toe ring—especially if she has the authority to place a "psych hold" on you to keep you from inflicting yourself on your workplace colleagues.

I removed the toe ring and stored it in my shirt pocket.

But later in the day I found yet another use for it when I had a chance encounter at the nurses' station with a twelve-year-old patient. The nurses were trying to cheer her up, but she seemed determined to find nothing amusing.

I asked her if she liked toe rings.

She did.

"Would you like to have one?" I asked.

She would.

I removed the ring from my pocket and swabbed it with alcohol.

"Here ya go. Good as new," I promised, offering it to her.

She kept her hands at her side as if to ask, *How come you had to clean it?*

I held it out, and she took it briefly in her hand, but she still wasn't smiling. By now, I really needed some help to get out of this awkward gift-giving situation. Fortunately, I got some.

"Chaplain," one of the nurses interrupted with a question out of the blue, "could you marry me?" Knowing she wanted me to perform the wedding, but relieved to be released from the hot seat, I couldn't resist having a little fun with this commonly misspoken request.

Turning to the patient, I momentarily took back the toe ring and extended it toward the nurse, saying, "Well, I do have a ring, but I should tell you I'm already happily married."

The nurse and the child looked at each other for a brief moment and then burst into a chorus of laughter.

Toe Ring Lesson #4: toe rings don't make good wedding rings, but they *can* be useful in getting acquainted.

I never would have thought that a toe ring could teach life lessons, but already I had learned four of them. And I was beginning to see at least two spiritual lessons developing as well.

First, while I don't usually recommend the practice of re-gifting, I suspect that the best gifts we can give are recycled ones. And by that I mean that our individual lives are a gift from God, and they are best enjoyed in recycling them to others in ways that show our own vulnerabilities.

Second, I meet a lot of people who like to tell me what a tough job I have, but the truth is that you don't need a seminary degree to be a minister. You don't have to know theology. You just need to know that God works through individuals who are willing to recycle themselves and give themselves away as God's gift to all. Because at the end of the day, it will never be about the faith you keep—it will always be about the faith you give.

A CANDY BAR BLESSING

"Today's the day I start the big diet," I told my wife as I raised my hand and promised, "No chocolate today!"

"Oh, has the hospital gift shop stopped selling Three Musketeers bars?" she asked, referring to my favorite candy bar.

"No," I said, letting my belt out an extra notch. "I'll just have to rely on some willpower."

But when I arrived at the hospital and found my little friend Benton had been admitted again, I knew my candy pledge would quickly melt. Because if Benton had things his way, and he usually did, I'd be eating a piece of candy from the bottomless bag he constantly shared.

Benton Regello was an eight-year-old boy who was blinded by a tumor when he was fifteen months old. For the next twenty-six months, he was in and out of our hospital for chemotherapy and surgeries. During that time, he made countless friends. Struck by his incredible bravery and resilience, our staff began to believe that Benton was going to beat his disease. "He was just a regular little boy," recalled one of the nurses, "only he learned his ABCs in braille."

For nearly four years, it seemed as though Benton *was* beating the odds, until one Friday afternoon in April 2003, when he developed a headache and lost movement on his right side. His mom rushed him to the hospital, where tests revealed a large tumor had hemorrhaged and caused a stroke. But the worst news was that the malignancy had spread into other areas of the brain.

Over the next several months, Benton came to our hospital many more times. Each time he came, he wandered the halls, guided by his mother. Each time one of his caregivers would say hello, Benton answered the greeting by dipping into his candy sack and holding out Hershey's Kisses. Sort of a trick or treat in reverse.

So, on that first day of my diet, I went to his room expecting more candy kisses. Instead, I found Benton curled up in his bed, his eyes open but not looking into this world. His parents, Bob and Jeanne, had moved their bed next to his and lay stretched alongside him, stroking his head and whispering things I could not hear.

Benton had suffered more seizures. And now he was dying.

"We've tried to say our good-byes," his mom explained. "But I know he's worried about us. He knows he's going to heaven, but he doesn't want to go there alone. Chaplain, could you say a prayer that he won't feel alone?"

My prayer came from Psalm 139:7–8:

> *Where can I go from your Spirit?*
> *Where can I flee from your presence?*
> *If I go up to the heavens, you are there.*

After the prayer, I helped the parents recall the days we'd seen him in the hospital giving out candy.

"We brought his candy bag with us. Would you like to have some?" Jeanne asked.

Without a mention of my diet, I reached into the bag and pulled out the first piece my fingers touched. When I opened my hand, I found a miniature version of a Three Musketeers.

The gravity of my tears was impossible to resist. It seemed as though Benton had saved one last piece of my favorite candy.

I managed some quick good-bye hugs and put the little

candy bar in my breast pocket. At home that evening, as I was getting undressed I removed the candy just as the phone rang. It was Benton's nurse.

"Thought you'd like to know, Chaplain. Benton passed away ten minutes ago," she said.

As I hung up the phone, I ripped open the half-melted candy bar and, with the solemnity of communion, I ate it.

Thanks, Benton. I'll start my diet tomorrow.

Part 2

"Chaplain to the ER, Stat!"

The pediatric unit isn't the only place where I encounter families and their children. Sometimes I meet them in the emergency room. For some parents, these frightening visits are nothing more than a wake-up call to reality. For others, it's the last place they see their children alive.

Forgive the rhyme, but there's a lot of drama in trauma. And to be honest, the folks who work in the ER like that drama—not the heartache that sometimes occurs there but the challenge to assuage it, the rush to fix broken bodies or at least to stabilize them until other specialists can mend the lives the ER staff has yanked back from the breach.

I admit there's part of me that likes that drama as well. Even during my clinical training at the University of California Davis Medical Center in Sacramento, I found the work in the ER so meaningful and compelling that soon my colleagues had playfully nicknamed me "the ambulance-chasing chaplain."

Despite the stressful and serious nature of their work, ER personnel laugh a lot. But their humor isn't often understood. It's a gallows-style humor that helps them deal with the tragedies they witness. I've seen them do seemingly callous things, such as collect bets on the blood-alcohol level of the drunk they're treating. And, out of the patients' hearing, I've heard them make jokes about those whose injuries resulted from certain "risk-related behaviors." (Trust me, you don't want to know what those behaviors are.)

But there's one thing I've never seen them joke about, one thing that will nearly always cause them to call in "outside help." That one thing is the death or life-threatening injury of a child. When it comes to children, the manager of the emergency unit will often call for reinforcements. That's when I hear the words, "Chaplain to the ER, stat!"

EVERY AVAILABLE RESPONSE

Before a child ever sees an emergency room, many of them (and their parents) will likely meet an emergency response worker, usually called a first responder. It was my own meeting with some first responders that led me to find my calling among health-care workers. That calling began in 1989 in an unlikely place: the Thursday afternoon quilting group at Berea Baptist Church in Stockton, California. I was the pastor of the church, and no, I don't quilt. But in addition to their beautiful quilts the ladies made fabulous cinnamon rolls, and, you know, someone had to be there to pray for the food, right?

The road leading to my calling came as I was leaving the quilters' potluck lunch and encountered a woman particularly given to histrionics.

"Pastor, did you hear about the man shooting at elementary school kids?" she asked excitedly.

"No," I said, "sounds horrid." But, considering the source, I let the subject revert to next week's potluck, er, quilting session, and then said my good-byes.

A few minutes away from the church's driveway, I began sensing that I had too easily dismissed the woman's report. I turned on the radio to hear reports of a massive emergency response at a nearby elementary school, where scores of students had been shot by a man with an automatic weapon. Having been recently trained to provide pastoral care for mass casualties, I naively considered myself prepared—and veered off toward the school.

Minutes later I was offering the on-scene commander my assistance as a local pastor with training in trauma pastoral care. He paused only a moment before sending me into a room where parents and counselors had been told to wait for a list of names that would be coming from the admitting hospitals. I found a seat next to an immigrant mother and her adolescent son. She didn't speak English, but I think somehow she knew the room was a kind of ruse. The other parents still seemed hopeful, but the counselors knew we were only awaiting final confirmation of the deaths.

We did not wait long. Soon the list came, but without an interpreter for the mother, I had few options. I held the list in front of her, placed my finger on what I assumed was her daughter's name, squeezed my lips together as if to hold back the terrible words, and shook my head sadly.

The woman recognized her daughter's name and asked, "Sh-di?"

I did not quite understand her, and our eyes collided with a pained look of confusion.

"Sh-di?" she repeated.

Seeing me squint as I attempted to understand, she echoed her question a third time, a little slower. "She *die*?" she said, with the raised tone of a question.

This time I understood. "Yes," I said, looking into her stoic face. "She die, yes. I'm so sorry. She die."

Her eyes swept the room, searching for a second opinion, but received only a confirming nod from her son. She did not cry. Neither she nor her son even moved. But suddenly, in something that can only be described as a sort of emotional ventriloquism, her own grief seemed to squeeze through her son's eyes, and a small tear traced a path along his frozen face. My memory of that woman and her son ends there. Perhaps they left very quickly after that.

But in stark contrast to the boy's single tear, the tears of the school's staff flowed for many days without ceasing. Teachers cried for the students and for their heroic colleague who was injured while shielding children from the hail of bullets. The principal cried for the children she had held as they bled out.

I cried too, overcome with the paralyzing dreadfulness of the event. The paralysis was so complete that later, when administrators asked for volunteers to complete a brief training class on counseling children, I did not raise my hand. I could not volunteer. The horror of what had happened had put a crack in my soul bigger than the entire school yard.

Yet as a Leonard Cohen song reminds us, "light gets in" through the cracks. Over the next several months, God's light began to filter through the cracks and guide me into two of the most fulfilling purposes I have yet known. The humbling confrontation with my own fears of inadequacy started a fire in my heart that grew into a full-blown calling, and eighteen months later, I began my training to become the hospital chaplain I am today. But perhaps even better than that, the horror and hopelessness I felt over being unable to save any of those children somehow translated into my finding another way to help children—through adoption.

One year after the tragedy at that elementary school, my wife and I started the process that would eventually welcome three new children—all siblings—into our home. The children we adopted weren't connected to the school shootings in any earthly way. And yet they were powerfully connected to the light that had begun to leak back into my heart in the months after the shooting.

God certainly had nothing to do with causing the tragedy at the school, but I am wholly convinced that he had everything to do with the rebuilding of lives after the tragedy.

Including mine.

IT TAKES A CHILD TO RAISE A VILLAGE

Keeping your religion while single-handedly getting small children ready for church is no small miracle. It can become a theological juggling act capable of tripping up even the most devout among us. Just waking a "tweenager" in time to shower is a miracle that's nothing short of beckoning the dead back to life. But when you add a preschool son who'd rather be chasing lizards with a first-grade daughter who insists on doing her own hair, your prayers will increase exponentially as you ask for a small miracle that will get you to the church on time.

But to truly appreciate the miracle of this morning madness, you have to mix in a wife who's out of town on a Sunday when you are filling in for an out-of-town pastor while simultaneously being on call at the hospital. Such was my crisis several years ago as the phone rang on that crazy Sunday morning.

"Good morning," I said, morphing into my best maitre d' voice.

The voice on the other end of the line didn't even pause for pleasantries: "Chaplain, we need you in the ER." I was the hospital's only chaplain—and on this day was without child care—so my supervisor had told me ahead of time I could decline any call that might be grossly inconvenient. While employed by that hospital I'd had to exercise that option only a few times, but this would have to be one of those times.

I started to explain the conflict that would keep me from helping when she interrupted me.

"Please!" she said briskly, an urgent tone rising in her voice.

I dropped the phone to my lap momentarily while I rethought my morning. "I suppose I could . . ."

She was in no mood to hear my child-care plan. "Please, Chaplain, just come. It's a bad one."

Her last sentence was redundant. I knew it had to be a serious situation. ER nurses don't use the P word if the trauma isn't bad.

A call to a neighbor found haven for my kids, and soon I was pushing through the first set of doors outside the ER. For a brief moment, I was insulated there between the two sets of doors, separated from the southern humidity outside and the wails of family members inside.

As the second set of doors opened, my first impression was that an entire church had assembled in the ER's waiting room. There were suits and scarves, hats and handkerchiefs, Bibles and bulletins. Only the pews and preacher were missing. Unable to tell the players without a scorecard, a triage nurse gave me the rundown: "Drunk driver 1, kid 0." Then she drew in a breath and added, "Room 19."

Room 19 was where we always put someone who had "expired." The word most of us commonly use for out-of-date medicines or magazine subscriptions takes on a different meaning in the ER. There, it is a word staff members use, perhaps to insulate themselves from the possibility that someday it could be their loved one in Room 19.

Making my way past secondary relatives and friends, I slipped unnoticed into the room, which was packed with more immediate family members. I paused reverently at the doorway until a break in the sobbing allowed an opening for an introduction. "I'm the hospital chaplain," I said. The crowd parted, and I was ceremoniously motioned toward the gurney to lead a prayer. "Is your minister here?" I asked.

"Our senior pastor is at church, but you're looking at one of our assistant ministers," a man said as he tossed his eyes toward the gurney. Thinking that the man had given the boy more of an honorary title, I shifted my thoughts toward a prayer. But my words disintegrated in my throat as I looked at the unforgettable sight of the small, seemingly unbroken figure of a nine-year-old boy.

Even now, years later, I distinctly remember how this child's body was missing the very things that define little boys—movement and energy. The nursery rhyme says little boys are so wiggly and squirmy they're described as being made of "snips and snails and puppy dog tails." This was probably a boy whose life once had been anything but still; he had moved, yearned, and inspired.

"He won't ever preach again," his dad muttered sadly to me.

Doubt gushed from my firmly blinking eyes. "Preach?" I blurted out.

"Oh yes," he said, "he's been preaching since he was six. He spent countless hours playing church until his mom finally asked our pastor for an opportunity to let the boy preach."

Child preachers were a part of this family's religious tradition, which didn't squelch the religious interests of children. Children became an expressive part of worship that was heard by all congregants.

I imagine that some would find fault with what seemed to be a tyranny of religious expectations on this boy's life. But the critics would also be compelled to acknowledge that many people wait all their lives to find their calling, while this little boy knew his calling early and expressed it until his last breath. And now, miraculously, even after his last breath, the little preacher continued to inspire the faithful to worship. Out in the waiting room, the congregation remained to sing "just one more song."

After excusing myself to pick up my children from the neighbor's house, I considered my earlier efforts at practically dragging my kids to church compared with this little preacher who had somehow managed to drag an entire church family behind him.

It's been said that it takes a village to raise a child, but on this day I had been privileged to witness a child miraculously and single-handedly raise up his own village.

SUICIDE—A RAFTING TRIP INTO WHITE-WATER TEARS

If I had the magical powers Charles Dickens conjured up in *A Christmas Carol*, I'd take every teenager I know back to a real afternoon when I waited for two frantic parents to arrive at the emergency room of the hospital where I worked. In my fantasy, I'd play the role of the ghost of Christmas future and huddle with the kids in a corner of the waiting room. We would gaze into the souls of the frightened parents as they came through the doors. As the ghost of the future, I would show them the pain they could cause their parents by taking their own life.

"Ya'll have my son?" the father asked loudly as he pushed through the doors.

"Yes, we do," the nurse answered. "The doctor's waiting."

That's a bad sign. Doctors don't usually wait.

It's even worse when the chaplain's there too. And I was.

I followed as she led the couple to the family room, and the doctor solemnly began unpacking the afternoon's events: "At 1:45 this afternoon, your son was found hanging from a tree in the local park. He was brought in without pulse or respiration. We worked on him for forty minutes before pronouncing him dead. I'm so sorry."

There. Right there. Freeze that frame, I would order the teenagers in my imaginary group as I looked into the eyes of those parents. If I could be the ghost of the future, I would shrink all the world's teenagers to microscopic size and take them on a rafting trip into their parents' white-water tears.

When these parents' tears finally slowed, their questions surged. And as each one was answered, unhealthy shame began to mold their faces. Seeing their agony, I wanted to beg the doctors to try one more time to resuscitate this kid.

"Something was wrong," the mother said. "We told him we loved him. Why couldn't he believe that?"

Freeze frame.

The accusing stares began, unintentional but noticed. I could even feel some of them welling up within me before I caught myself and quickly changed gears. The police and medical staff began asking what seemed like prosecutorial questions about what the parents knew and when. Perhaps the questioners wanted to assure themselves that no matter how frustrating things were with their own children, things could never reach these proportions.

My eyes sought to stare down each inquisitor. *Yes, this could be your kid. Yes, nurse, your sweet Suzie, and yes, Doc, your smart Ivy League Billy. This could be your kid.*

"Can we see him?" the parents asked.

"Yes," the nurse said, "the chaplain will take you back."

Entering the room, I turned away. I made sure my eyes didn't find the kid. I was plenty mad at him, even if his parents weren't. Mom's hand found his face and cupped his cheek in her palm. "Baby," she sobbed as if summoning him from the dead. "Baby, we loved you. We loved you so much!"

Then she turned to me. "We tried to tell him that. How come he didn't know it?" she asked.

"Did you hate me that much?" the dad pleaded with his boy. "I loved you. I know I didn't show it, but I did."

If I could just convince myself this family was messed up, I thought, I could distance myself from their senseless pain. But the parents seemed pretty normal, and that was the scariest part. In this country, *normal* means that for every two homicides in the United States, there are three suicides.

Psychologist Karl Menninger taught that suicide was "murder 180 degrees." He meant that the person who dies from suicide kills the image of something he hates that is reflected in him. The suicide victim wants to murder someone or some image but cannot, so he chooses instead to permanently close his own eyes to that thing he hates.

On that tragic afternoon, Menninger's theory seemed right. This kid had just murdered every bit of joy these parents had ever known in having a son. He had murdered every dream, hope, wish, and future this couple had ever held for him.

As they left our ER, it felt as if there had been not a single suicide but three murders.

In Dickens's story, as the ghost of Christmas future brings Scrooge to his own tombstone, Scrooge demands that the ghost "answer me one question. Are these the shadows of the things that will be, or are they shadows of things that may be, only?"

The ghost doesn't answer but continues pointing toward the grave.

"Men's courses will foreshadow certain ends, to which, if persevered in, they must lead," Scrooge says. "But if the courses be departed from, the ends will change."

What grief would have been prevented had that sixteen-year-old boy departed from the course that brought him, and his parents, to such a tragic end.

Suicide is the second-leading cause of death among college students and third among youth ages fifteen to twenty-four. Talking to someone about suicide does not encourage the act. If you suspect a friend or loved one has these feelings, ask directly whether he or she is considering hurting him or herself and how it might be done. Look for stressors such as abuse, humiliating events, a loss such as a breakup with a boyfriend or girlfriend, failure in school, or a death or divorce in the family. If you are the person who's thinking about committing suicide, call the national referral network at 1-800-SUICIDE (784-2433).

IN THE TWINKLING OF AN EYE

I planned my escape to the last detail. I needed to leave Disney World with rent money. But then I spotted him—the one last Disney vendor strategically placed between the tram and me. Too late. He shoved an inflated, big-eared rat in my daughter's face, and the giant sucking sound heard was the grocery money leaving my wallet.

OK, OK. I bought her the balloon. But I warned her, If you lose this one, you won't get a new one. The balloon was so big it needed its own tram seat, and we barely managed to get back to our parking space. Then, as we were getting into our car, our daughter let out a blood-curdling scream. She had lost her balloon.

What is the strong pull balloons have on little girls? Whatever it is, some keep the fascination long after childhood. It was that fascination, on an early morning several years ago, that led a young woman to stop her car on the side of an elevated freeway to watch a blimp float across the sky. The college-age girl decided to take a picture of the blimp as it passed overhead. In the instant it took her to focus the camera, a semitruck swerved slightly to avoid a road hazard and found no resistance in the slight frame of the blimp-watching girl.

She was dead at the scene; but with victims this young, emergency responders often send the bodies to the hospital anyway because first responders are ill equipped to make death notifications. In contrast, most hospitals have social workers and chaplains who can support the family and help make necessary arrangements.

The ER clerk gave me the girl's name and told me the mother had been called but had not been given any additional information. I was told to wait at the door and watch for "Mrs. Stephens."

I didn't know Mrs. Stephens, but I knew what she would look like. She would look like all of us would look if we were called at the office and told, "There's been an accident involving your daughter. The doctors are with her now. Can you come to the hospital?"

The ER had unexpectedly filled with police officers, so I didn't notice when a female officer hurried past me to the front desk. But then I heard her say, "I'm Mrs. Stephens. You have my daughter."

Oh, God! I thought—a prayer, not just an exclamation. *How can I do this?*

"Mrs. Stephens," I began, putting on a professional air, "I'm the chaplain. Please come with me." I did a pivot and bolted forward, but a jerk to my shoulder reversed my momentum.

"No!" she said as she swung me around. "Tell me right here." Squarely facing me, she grabbed my shoulders with both hands. "Just tell me what happened. Is my daughter OK? Just tell me!" she ordered.

My reasoning had become a bit incoherent and cowardly. Perhaps the gun she wore rattled me and made me a bit more disposed to follow her orders. "No, ma'am," I answered quickly. "She's not OK. She died."

Grabbing at my suit coat, she slid down my torso like a woman sliding off a cliff. "Nooooooo!" she screamed.

Only a few hours earlier this mother had kissed her daughter good-bye, not knowing it was the last time she would see her alive. In an instant, a daughter's life was snuffed out and a mother's life was forever changed.

She asked to see her daughter. We tried to discourage her, explaining in the gentlest way we could that her daughter was badly "broken." But she persisted. And as she determinedly entered the room, she quickly dissolved into wails of despair interspersed with staccato sentences telling us she recently lost her police-officer brother in a duty-related shooting.

There is something about balloons that reinforce that cliché about the only love "meant to be" is the love that returns to you after you release it. As parents, we nurture and protect our children as long as possible. But the time comes when we have to let them go, knowing that the possibility exists that we may be faced with inexplicable unfairness. We may get a call someday summoning us to an emergency room where we must endure a loss that tears our heart in two. At such a time we probably hope, as first responders do, that there's somewhere—or Someone—else we can send our grief to, to help us get through what's coming.

My own daughter found a great way to keep her favorite balloons. She denied them any flight at all—deflated them and tacked them to a wall in a display that resembled wanted posters in the Disney post office.

Just like my daughter did, we can also deny our children flight, at least for a while. But when we do, at some point the resistance ceases, and the children no longer resemble the love that originally inflated them. Pin the child to the wall, and she becomes a trophy, protected and safe; but a trophy does not love.

By the way, I couldn't make good on my original threat. I did buy another Mickey balloon, and the truth was, we still had food money. Now my daughter has a car, and it seems like I rarely see her, but when I do catch a glimpse of her, she is almost always flying high!

THE COST OF LOVE

Seeing a sign promising ten-dollar roses, my guilty conscience conspired with my cheapskate heart, and I swerved my car into the florist's parking lot. I swaggered into the shop and asked the man behind the counter, "How much are your Valentine roses?"

"For which day?" he asked.

Now, I'm thinking, *If this man doesn't know which day is Valentine's Day, he's having a bigger career crisis than this chaplain can help him with. Either that, or he has mistaken me for someone who plans a year in advance.*

I bet on the latter probability and replied, "Valentine's Day, this year."

"Yes, but which day of the week?" he asked.

"The day of the week that Valentine's Day falls on," I answered, as if this were a trick question.

"Well," he said, "Valentine's Day is Thursday, but roses are cheaper on Monday. We get market price for them on the big day."

Imagine seeing the gears of a truck shifting just before it runs you over. That's what I imagined was going on in the florist's head as I took the bait. "What's the price on Thursday?" I asked. The guilty husband and the penny pincher in me were at war.

"Seventy dollars—supply and demand," he said, smiling apologetically as I grimaced.

"Hmmm," I mused as I walked backward toward the door like a sheriff cornered by some bad banditos in a border-town saloon. "Thank ya kindly, sir," I added, staying in the western script.

My hesitant retreat was doing nothing to slow his lecture on the laws of economics. "This is the best price you'll find," he said in the pleading tone of a street vendor.

Man! I thought. *How much is love supposed to cost?*

Scripture defines the highest price a person can pay for love. John 15:13 says, "Greater love has no one than this, that he lay down his life for his friends."

That's quite a price. It makes seventy-dollar roses seem like a bargain.

I know of people who've shown that kind of love, either deliberately or accidentally. I've met some of them—or their families—in hospital emergency rooms.

Several years ago I sought to comfort the family of a seventeen-year-old boy who had been pronounced dead after our emergency room staff had done everything they could to save him. Employed at a local Houston water park, he and his co-workers were playing after-hours volleyball at the park when one of the employees decided to see how far he could shimmy up a light pole. As the light pole began to sway, the climber jumped clear, but the pole continued its threatening gyrations and then began a slow descent toward the gamers. Seeing that the pole was about to hit a friend, our patient shoved the friend out of danger and then shielded his own body with outstretched hands. Tragically, the tottering pole had lost its electrical ground and as the boy "caught" it, he fielded 220 volts. Neither the valiant attempts of his grieving lifeguard friends nor any of the efforts by paramedics and hospital staff ever gave this boy another breath on his own.

For the next few hours, hospital staff made repeated attempts to contact the parents, until finally the cryptic message asking them to come to the hospital reached them. As they arrived, I mentioned our many attempts to reach them, and their reply stopped us all cold. They had been at a nearby cancer center, they said, where their oldest son was dying of leukemia.

After the doctor explained the events of their son's death and our attempts to resuscitate him, his co-workers gathered to praise his heroic sacrifice. Looking for words that would bring closure for them, I noted how remarkable it was that he had given his life for his friend.

The hero's mother deflected my remarks and changed the subject. But in my naiveté, I pushed on, quoting John 15:13. She thanked me kindly "for the sentiments" and added, "I'm sure that will be of comfort to me someday, but right now, you'll have to excuse me if I wish it was some other boy in that morgue and not my son."

For love to be complete, the sacrifice of love has to be accepted. The friend whose life had been saved undoubtedly accepted the sacrifice, but the mother of the boy who made it could not. Knowing she had reared a brave son who would "lay down his life for his friends" didn't ease her pain. Not yet anyway.

The events of that day made me think about another time when a supreme sacrifice was made. Christians are called to honor the unimaginable sacrifice Jesus made on our behalf. Only as we accept that sacrifice can God's love complete its intended gesture.

No matter how much I spent on roses that week before Valentine's Day—even if I maxed out my Visa and worked two jobs to pay the balance—my love could only be filled as my wife accepted the sacrifice I offered.

After leaving the florist shop that day, I called my wife at work. "You know I love you more than seventy dollars, right?"

"Yeah," she said, her answer unsuccessfully masking her suspicion. "I suppose so."

"The roses are seventy dollars!"

"What roses?"

"Valentine's Day roses!"

"That's crazy," she said, releasing an exhausted breath. "Forget about it!"

"But you know I love you more than that, right?"

"Yes," she cooed. "I know you love me more than that." Then she paused. "You can buy me roses for my birthday next month—they'll be cheaper then."

And with that comment, we reached an agreement on this year's market price of love.

THE HOUSEGUEST

Words can take on different meanings in different locations. After my family finished a big meal in a London restaurant, my teenager leaned back to pat her bloated stomach and announced very loudly, "I'm stuffed," causing other patrons to raise their eyebrows, questioning the appropriateness of her announcement telling these Londoners she was with child.

Another word with various definitions is *houseguest*. It should mean "a welcomed visitor." However, in our California home, it usually means the in-laws are coming to drag us and their grandchildren to Disneyland or Fisherman's Wharf, all while looking at time-shares that offer potential customers free luggage or a cruise. (Generally I urge the in-laws to make the cruise a matter of "prayerful consideration.")

Yes, *houseguest* can be a dirty word, but I would never have realized just how harsh a word it could become until one memorable night in a hospital ER. Radioed reports from inbound EMTs told us a family of stab victims were minutes from arrival. The family had welcomed a houseguest who, without their knowledge, used crack cocaine. Somewhere in the middle of the darkest night this family would ever know, the man depleted both his source of crack and apparently his sanity as well. Wanting the former but badly needing the latter, he demanded money from the family members and attacked anyone who resisted. For him, it was "time to kill."

As our ER team triaged the victims, it became apparent that the dad had already died, the baby was straining between this world and the next, the mom was stable (*stable* being a relative word in such a situation), and the ten-year-old "big sister" was physically OK but had a traumatized psyche suspended some-where between logical-and-in-control and "whacked out."

The staff asked me to watch the ten-year-old so they could work with the mom and baby; I offered her the solace of the hospital chapel and was a bit surprised when she agreed to go with me. As soon as we settled in, she began praying, asking God to help her family recover. "Please make everything OK," she said. "Amen." But then she added a PS, using words not usually employed around a chaplain. She demanded to know why God had let her father die. She had a few choice words for the family's houseguest as well.

Experts usually say that trauma victims who are able to debrief within twenty-four hours of an incident are more likely to recover faster. So I let her continue her angry tirade. But when she swept the candles off the altar and started overturning chairs, I called for help. Jeannie, a nursing supervisor, answered the call. She had not only worked her share of tragedy, but she also knew personal tragedy.

She placed her arms around the distraught child in much the same way I had seen her place her arms around her own son who had been left paralyzed by an auto accident the year before. She brought the girl back to the ER, where a common allergy medicine helped her rest and begin the healing process.

I've learned that sometimes the most difficult moments of my work as chaplain impart the most lasting lessons. The tragic things I saw that day helped me have a new understanding of the word *houseguest* and how that understanding can affect the way we live. The word can have different meanings. Sometimes it means on-the-go in-laws, and sometimes it means a wel-comed friend. But it can also define that part of us that invites the unimaginable into our lives. The murderous houseguest who attacked this family had invited an unimaginably evil "houseguest" into his life. It was a substance that awakened the ugliest part of him and urged him to do the unspeakable.

In the end, the little girl realized that she, too, had a choice of houseguests. She could invite into her life the reincarnation of the anger that killed her father, but by doing so she would become part of the reflection of her father's killer. Her other choice was to invite a houseguest that would initiate a time for healing.

We, too, choose our emotional and spiritual houseguests. Ideally, we welcome good things into our life. In his letter to the Philippians, the apostle Paul listed the best houseguests to have: "Fix your thoughts on what is true and honorable and right. Think about things that are pure and lovely and admirable. Think about things that are excellent and worthy of praise. Keep putting into practice all you learned from me and heard from me and saw me doing, and the God of peace will be with you" (4:8–9 NLT).

A DELICATE BALANCE

So far in my job as a chaplain, I've never had to risk performing my duties "under fire." That is, unless you count the time I physically shielded a doctor from the angry fists of a man accusing the doctor of caring too much about profits at our "for-profit" hospital. Then there was the time (I'll tell you about it a little later) I "pulled rank" on an army sergeant to prevent him from dislocating his wife's shoulder. I guess those were pretty dangerous situations, but neither had me fearing for my life.

Most of us do our everyday jobs with no need to take many risks, in part because our culture has made safety an art form. We do everything possible to protect ourselves from death. From an early age, we learn fire prevention, drug avoidance, stranger awareness, and pedestrian safety. And once we hit puberty, we learn contraception, rape prevention, and AIDS awareness. We host prevention conventions. We wear hard hats, helmets, and seat belts. We take classes in smoking cessation, self-defense, defensive driving, and CPR. We read books on diet, exercise, and stress management.

But safety cannot be guaranteed, despite our most careful precautions. I learn that anew each time I'm called to the emergency room. I remember especially a couple who came rushing in with their three-year-old son. They had done all the right things to keep their son safe but had been blindsided by a danger they could never have anticipated.

As always, the staff greeted the devastated parents with questions, probably expecting to detect shortcomings. Surely the boy's mother had let him out of her sight, or his father had left him in the yard without watching him properly. *Humph! Parents who don't watch their kids!* we all probably thought self-righteously.

We were good at playing twenty questions with the families of trauma patients. You see, if we could identify at least two or three stupid things the victim or the parents had done, then we could assure ourselves that there was no way anything that stupid or tragic could ever happen to us. We would never be that careless or reckless or dumb.

But that night the facts began to diffuse our judgmental attitude. (Facts are tricky that way.) The mom had taken her son on a play date to a beautifully swept tennis court in an exclusive metropolitan suburb. The court was gated, locked, supervised, cleaned, and staffed by background-checked employees.

Tempted by the smooth, wide surface, the boy asked, "Can I take off my shoes, Mommy?"

"Sure," she replied, perhaps remembering how good cool concrete can feel to bare feet.

The boy then set about exploring his environment. He began kicking at the tennis-court fence. *This is fun. I'm in a giant playpen with Mommy,* he may have thought. It was safe. There was no way out and no way for anyone else to get in without passing Mom. And if any trouble did come, Mom was close enough to meet it.

Close enough, but not fast enough. Barefooted, the youngster kicked a place on the fence near an outdoor outlet that was not properly grounded, a condition that caused that section of fence to become electrified. The tennis court was damp from a morning rain, and when the boy's damp, bare foot touched the fence, his life spirit left his body in as little time as it takes to flip a light switch.

Hearing what had happened caused many of the ER staff to realize uncomfortably, *There was nothing I would have done differently. This could have been my child.*

How can we balance our need for safety with our need to live freely and enjoy what life's blessings, such as children, can bring? If we fill our days with extraordinary efforts to prevent injury and death—our own or our loved ones'—we'll miss the abundant life God intends for us to live daily. If we keep our children constantly confined to a small, safe room where they can never be hurt—where they can never feel the cool, pleasant dampness of an outdoor tennis court after a morning rain—we aren't just protecting them. We're imprisoning them; indeed, we might be accused of abusing them by our own good intentions.

Death has always been undeniably closer than we think.

Scripture teaches us that "it is appointed unto men once to die, but after this the judgment" (Hebrews 9:27 KJV). The teaching admonishes us not only to be ready to meet our God but, it seems to me, also to live our lives the way we would if we knew with certainty that death is coming tomorrow for us or for our loved ones.

There is no way we can permanently prevent death, and the fear of it must not stop us from living or from allowing our children to carefully discover and enjoy the world around them. We do our best to protect ourselves and our families, always aware that death is close, but life can be closer.

I urge you to choose life.

Part 3

GROWN-UP MIRACLES

Although most of my hospital work occurs in pediatric units or in labor and delivery, I also find myself occasionally tending those in need of pastoral care in other parts of the medical facility—or in other parts of the country. Like the littlest hospital patients, grown-up patients have stories, too, and in those stories, miracles abound.

DISTRACTIONS CLOUD PURPOSE

If you're younger than forty, you may never have heard of Gidget and her true love, Moondoggie. So you may find it hard to understand why I would bring home the video production of their beachside love story. That's OK; my children didn't understand either.

It was a time I'd been a little worried about them; my son had a broken foot, and another one of our teenagers was having trouble with grades. Maybe we could watch a video together and take our minds off those worrisome issues for a while, I thought. And what better way to divert our minds than watching a "family" movie together?

Gidget is the mother of all surf movies. If you want to know how the Gidget character sounded, just imagine a preteen girl babbling away to her friends. And if you want to know what Gidget looked like, imagine a *Baywatch* babe surfing in your grandmother's girdle.

Get the picture? My kids did, so it was no surprise they were thrilled when my pager went off in the middle of the movie, saving them from gagging on surf. *Gidget* would have to wait while I headed to the hospital to meet a real-life Gidget—a grieving, older Gidget who had lost her true love.

I found her in a hospital room lit only with the glow of the flat-line heart monitor. Alone, talking at Gidget speed, she was massaging the hands of an elderly man she had been dating. Her "Moondoggie." Her feelings of aloneness came through in a roaring rush of words as she expressed concern for her boyfriend's eternal aloneness.

"He didn't believe in God. I tried to tell him—to warn him— 'You've got to believe!'" she said.

"He's not alone," I answered, stroking her back and waiting for the nursing supervisor to pronounce the obvious.

Reaching over to push one of his eyelids up, she asked, "Is he really dead?"

"Yes," I said with a nod.

"I was just here with him. He said hello. I only lay down to sleep for about twenty minutes. I was so tired from my daily trips to visit him," she said, full of regret that she hadn't been with him at the end. "What am I going to do?"

On and on she went.

My sympathetic sounds encouraged her to keep going, and when the nurse arrived, she repeated it all over again to both of us. Unfortunately, both of us had places we needed to be. As a chaplain, sometimes I help out people, and sometimes I have to help people out. The supervisor signaled me this was one of those times, and I needed to encourage an ending.

"Did the taxi bring you here tonight?" I asked.

"Yes," she said, her eyes still focused on Moondoggie.

"Your boyfriend's nurse said she usually calls the taxi for you."

She paused. "Is it time to leave?"

"You have a lot to do tomorrow," I said.

"OK," she said. Then she picked up her purse and began to walk with me toward the door—all the while shooting questions over her shoulder to the nurses. As we stood outside waiting for the taxi, she continued talking at Gidget speed in an eternal loop. Deep in her heartache, her monologue was broadcasting a ping of distress, like a submarine using echolocation to find an ally. Sadly, she wasn't pinging on much—not even me.

I was alternating between caring about her struggle and worrying about my teenager's grades and my son's broken foot. But somewhere in the fog of my mental meandering, I connected with the echoes coming from her stories and her pings finally found me. I touched my hand to her face and brushed her cheek with the back of my fingers. Her hand came to meet mine, and soon both her hands were holding my hand.

Then things grew quiet. She stroked my hand as though she recognized she wasn't alone, and in a moment she broke the silence, whispering into my palm, "Your hand's so warm."

I smiled just as my pager beeped.

The sound stunned her for a moment, but then I saw understanding. "I guess other people need you too. Like me," she said.

"Probably," I answered, nodding toward the ER doors.

The taxi pulled up. The driver stepped out, opened the door wordlessly, watched her settle herself on the seat, then shut her in—alone. As the cab pulled away, I saw her silently mouth the words "thank you" through the window.

I raised my hand good-bye and realized it was really I who needed to thank her. I had almost let my own plans and problems distract me from my purpose—to be there, listen through the words, hear her heart, and reach out to take her hand.

Touched by her tenderness, after I responded to the page at the emergency room, I happened by Moondoggie's room. Seeing he was still there, I leaned through the door and felt myself give him a little wink, as if to say, *That's quite a gal you had there!*

LIP-SYNC PRAYERS

I've discovered something that chaplains and physical therapists (PTs) have in common—patients lie to us. Patients lie to PTs about exercising, and they lie to chaplains about church attendance.

How do I know people lie to PTs? you ask.

Uh, well, maybe because I'm not exactly forthcoming with mine.

"Did you do your neck stretches this week?" she asks.

"Uh, sure," I mumble as I avoid looking at her while pretending to stretch. "I stretch my neck every time I cross the street."

Like the PT, I'm often on the receiving end of these creative stories, especially when I ask patients where they get their spiritual strength. I want to find what connects them to a spiritual significance while I try to help them sort out their spiritual presuppositions about illness.

Eight times out of ten, they misinterpret my intent and exaggerate their church attendance. How do I know? Hey, if they can't remember their church's name or denomination or their pastor's name, they ain't been in a while! Usually, after I assure them I'm not their fourth-grade Sunday school teacher putting stars on an attendance chart, we get down to meaningful conversation.

Ironically, one of the most honest answers I got from a patient came from a man who didn't exaggerate anything. A military engineer, he was a heart patient at our hospital. When I asked him where he got his spiritual support, he answered, "I'm not sure I even believe in God."

"That's OK," I said. "I'm in customer service, not sales."

He liked that, and despite the fact that I didn't always relate to his engineer's mind, we managed to develop a friendship during the next year. We found common ground in talking about the future, about our children, about investing, and about how I could dampen the noise of that infernal train that ran through my subdivision.

One day, I stopped by his room for a quick visit after he'd been admitted for something routine. I left with assurances he'd be discharged soon. But "soon" grew into four weeks, and with each visit his condition seemed worse. One day, we found out why: he had cancer, and he wasn't going to get better.

Our next several visits turned from engineering and investing toward spiritual things. When he asked me what I thought about God, I looked surprised. I assumed he knew what I believed: Yes, there is a God. Yes, he is a loving God. And yes, he wants an up-close-and-personal relationship with us.

"OK, but I want to know what I should do with God in my situation," he said. "How do I approach him? I trust you to tell me."

"Going to God is just like talking to me. Just talk. Tell God you need to have a relationship," I answered.

He wasn't buying it. "I feel like a hypocrite," he said. "I've never talked to him before, and now, in the end, he's supposed to believe I'm sincere?"

"That's right. That's the way it works," I said, laying my hand on his shoulder.

"Really?"

"Yes. You may recall that Jesus was crucified between two revolutionaries who had killed and robbed for their cause. The first guy—I call him Dead Man Mocking—goaded Jesus to use magical powers to save them all. The other guy couldn't find any pride in the life he'd lived; in the last hours of his life, he sought a spiritual connection with Jesus. Jesus didn't rebuff his request because others might have seen it as hypocritical. Instead, he assured the man that his 'prayer' was answered; Jesus even told the man he would escort him to his spiritual home.

"With God," I concluded, "it doesn't matter what you've done with the past years of your life. It only matters what you're going to do with the next minute of your life."

"I don't think I can talk to God by myself. Can you do it for me?" he asked.

At this point, you need to understand that a chaplain's training is in reflective listening and presence. We don't do Ann Landers. We don't tell you how to solve your problem. We listen. Not so with this man. He wasn't asking for reflective listening; he was asking for spiritual intervention. He was asking me to take him to God.

As a hospital chaplain answering the requests of patients, I've done some fairly unorthodox things. I've taped crystals to wrists, turned a bed eastward, put a healing blanket on the bed and garlic under the bed. But nobody had ever asked me to lip-sync prayers. It was very unorthodox.

"OK," I agreed, "but if I pray something you don't agree with, squeeze my hand for a do-over."

As I did my best to prayerfully reflect my friend's intentions, the resulting prayer reminded me of the steadying hand I had offered my daughter as she first learned to walk. Now, this man wanted my prayers to steady him as he learned how to walk to God on his own. Suddenly, it seemed quite reasonable to be unorthodox.

As I left his room, I passed my physical therapist in the hall, holding out her arms to steady a wobbly patient. I suddenly felt the inspiration to return to my office, do my neck exercises, and say prayers of gratitude for all the helping hands in my life.

Three weeks after my visit, my engineer friend died. He had prayed for physical healing, but in the end found a different kind of healing. He found a newness in life that doesn't exist on this side of the curtain. Lip-sync prayers may not work for everyone, but they did for this man. He found that reaching out to God, in whatever form, is always met with a steady hand.

UNIMAGINABLE NEWS

If you've ever watched *Star Trek*, you would know that the crew members often find themselves in a place "where no man has gone before." When that happens, their instruments usually don't work. As much as they try to recalibrate everything, they inevitably lose the power to their protective shields. The same energy that is messing with their instruments may also be making crew members disappear one by one and causing parallel universes to crash, smash, and clash. In the place where no man has gone before, everything is out of whack.

In my experience, people experience similar confusion when they hear a doctor tell them their illness is inoperable. Their world contorts, and they're hit with spiritual vertigo. My work means that sometimes I'm invited into that contorted world. On this particular day, the call came from a nurse.

"Chaplain, we have a patient who's requesting that you come and pray with her," the nurse said. "Her doctor has just told her that she has another tumor and there's nothing more to be done."

After a quick briefing at the nurses' station, I entered the woman's room and introduced myself. "I understand you've gotten some unimaginable news today," I said. Even the word *unimaginable* seemed like an understatement. The thirty-three-year-old woman had been expecting great news from the recent medical tests. But instead of hearing that her cancer was in remission and that her three-year tour of duty in cancer's twilight zone had reached its conclusion, she heard, "You have a new tumor, and it's inoperable."

"I'm trying to be strong," she told me, "but I just can't stop crying."

Shaking my head, I wondered aloud whether I'd be able to stop either if I had just heard my doctor tell me I had inoperable cancer. "Is there a reason you have to stop?"

"Yes, I have to be strong for my mother. I'm all she has," the woman said. "She's been so strong since I got sick. She's my rock. It would destroy her to see me cry so much."

I often hear similar statements from patients who have a certain expectation of what "strong" is supposed to look like. These folks usually find tears to be shaming, embarrassing, or weak, and I suppose tears *can* sometimes indicate such things. But I've also seen great strength and courage in tears.

"Shielding yourself from your tears must take up a great deal of energy," I said, still thinking in *Star Trek* terms. "You might better use that energy in talking about your relationship with your mother and the other special people in your life, and even your relationship with God. Besides, you know your mother is going to cry when you're gone. Have you ever thought maybe she'd like to cry *with* you? Maybe she's waiting for your permission to cry."

"Mom's not cried since this whole thing began," she admitted.

"Maybe you've not seen her cry," I speculated. "My guess is, losing her only child has got to be devastating, and maybe she'd like the opportunity to express that."

I told her that the desire to express grief is something that her mother and God had in common. "Surely God must have cried when his only Son was killed," I said.

She looked at me quizzically.

"Doesn't the Bible teach that at the crucifixion, the earth went dark for three hours? I think your mom's world must be looking pretty dark too," I told her.

At that remark, her tears began to fall like water leaking from a paper sack.

My wife often tells me that I'm usually not satisfied at the end of a day's work if I haven't made someone cry. To which I always reply, "*Helped* someone cry—*helped*, not *made* them cry!"

This woman's cancer couldn't be cured. But I'd like to think that she and her mother experienced some emotional healing and a renewal of their relationship from the holy water of tears that fell from their eyes. Tears, I've learned, can renew the dry places inside us.

Shedding tears in the presence of a loved one may bring us into a place where none of us has gone before. But it's worth the trip. Dropping our protective shields and letting others see our tears shows them we trust them and we acknowledge their love for us. To share tears with another person is an act of supreme compassion. In holding back the tears, we hold back our truth. And when we're faced with our mortality, the only thing we have to share with each other is, ultimately, ourselves.

MAKING MAMA CRY

When people ask me what it takes to become a hospital chaplain I'm often tempted to come back with a pun that parodies a movie about fighter pilots and astronauts. "The Righteous Stuff," I want to answer.

If the person is serious, I usually tell him or her it takes school, work experience, and the successful completion of clinical pastoral education, a one-year clinical residency in which students visit patients under the mentoring direction of a gray-haired supervisor.

A seed of wisdom my supervisor once imparted to me seemed a bit odd at the time, but I've since come to appreciate its wisdom. "Sometimes," he said, "the only power a patient has left is the power to kick the chaplain out of the room. When you're a patient in the hospital, you can't kick the doctor or nurse out, unless you want to give up and die, but the chaplain can be dismissed with little negative effect."

I saw that seed come to fruition one day as I entered the crowded room of a woman who was being discharged from our hospital after undergoing a routine hysterectomy. But the morning had brought terrible news: her house had burned to the ground the previous night. Now the social workers and I were the proverbial "king's men," summoned to put her Humpty Dumpty world back together again.

I introduced myself as the hospital chaplain, then I simply grasped her hand and said, "This has been a pretty difficult day for you. I understand you received some terrible news."

Up to that point she had kept her composure, but upon hearing those words, her tears erupted in loud sobs. All she could do was nod her head.

As I've mentioned, my wife teases me that I have no job satisfaction unless I can make people cry. I keep telling her I *help* them cry—and I have a good reason for doing it. I talk to people about intimate matters, and when they want to deny their pain and suppress the tears, they give me "just the facts." But as they are given permission to safely share their story, trusting that they won't be ridiculed or criticized, the tears become the stream that carries the story. In my job, tears can be the only tangible indication that the truth is about to surface.

But not everyone is impressed with my skill to encourage tears. The tears of the woman whose house had burned brought a very tall and menacing nineteen-year-old man in my direction.

"Get out of here!" he roared.

"Pardon me?" I asked.

"You're making my mama cry!" he said accusingly.

Making? In my mind, I questioned his charge.

Still sobbing, the woman used one hand to direct her son out of the room and the other hand to anchor me to her side.

"Get out of here!" he repeated, ignoring her direction. "You can't come in here and make my mama cry."

"Maybe," I slowly and guardedly suggested, "I'm the only one who has come here today willing to give your mother *permission* to cry."

His mother nodded in more agreement, swiping at her tears, but my suggestion went right past him. He repeated his order and brandished his fist just out of his mother's view. My supervisor had been right: the son was exercising the only power he had left, and I was being dismissed.

"You!" his mom declared finally, "are the one who is leaving." The son hesitated a moment longer. "Right now!" she barked.

"Mama," he pleaded.

But Mama had the real power. "Now!" she ordered. "Right now before I have them call hospital security." With that, he found an exit, and I stayed while the social workers devised a new housing plan.

In the young man's efforts to suppress his mother's tears, he was actually telling her that their shared pain was too much for him. In one of my less-than-good chaplain moments, I wanted to ask him, "If she stops crying, will you feel better?"

Many of us seek to stop the tears of others with a "there, there" pat on the back or a quick hug before we let go and step back. Tears make many of us uncomfortable. We mistake the symptom of tears for the actual problem, and we wrongly believe we can dismiss the problem by dismissing the tears.

What would it take to become a chaplain? My guess is that it requires much of the same thing that is required to be a real person, an authentic friend. The message of the gospel is that we all need to be ministers. And sometimes, when the only power people have left is the power to express tears—or even aggressive anger—ministry can take place as we become willing to give emotion permission to be expressed.

A MIRACLE IN THE INPUT, IF NOT IN THE OUTCOME

In football, it's called a punt. In the hospital, it's a referral. It occurs when hospital staff members realize a patient's needs are beyond their responsibility or expertise; they know *they* can't do what's needed but hope that surely someone somewhere can do something.

Oftentimes I'm the "someone" they call to do "something."

Answering one of those calls, I bolted through the ER doors as Dolores, the charge nurse, threw an arm across my chest like a railroad crossing gate. "Chaplain, we've got a man here with the flu," she said, shifting into whisper mode, "and I thought maybe you could do something for his wife."

The look I gave Dolores must have shown that I didn't consider the flu serious enough to generate a chaplain referral. "It's serious, Norris," she said grimly. "He walked up to the triage desk on his own but began turning blue in the treatment room."

"OK, sounds serious, but what made you think his wife wanted a chaplain? Did she ask for one?" I asked.

"Not exactly," she said, pointing to a forty-eight-year-old woman sitting in a waiting area down the hall. The woman was mumbling to herself and looked more like a psych patient than a visitor as she rocked herself in a stationary chair.

As I got close enough to hear her, I realized she wasn't mumbling incoherent gibberish. She was praying.

"Help me, Jesus. Help me, Jesus. Oh, God! Please help me, Jesus," she said in a soft, urgent voice.

I put my hand on her shoulder and joined her chorus: "Help her, Jesus. Help her, please. Hear her cry."

She suddenly grabbed my hand and pulled me downward just as Dolores grabbed a nearby chair and slid it under me. The distraught woman and I were kneecap to kneecap.

"Is my husband going to live? I've told Jesus I'd do anything." She paused for just a moment before the words burst from her again in one long train of worry. "He only had a cold. We went to the doctor, he gave us some medicines, and then we came home. Three days later, he was looking much worse. I begged him to return to the doctor. 'Something's not right,' I told him. 'We should go back to the doctor.' But he argued that doctors would just tell him to drink plenty of liquids and get some rest. So we did nothing until this morning."

"What happened then?" I asked.

"His temperature wouldn't go down. He was hallucinating. He didn't know what day it was, and his temperature hit 105," she answered sadly.

Behind the woman's back, Dolores shook her head and raised a finger toward the roof to indicate a higher fever.

"Chaplain, what's going to happen? Is he going to live?" the woman asked sadly.

Revealing her answer only to me, Dolores shook her head in a definitive *no*. Then she disappeared back into the treatment room.

That's when I wanted to make a referral of my own. It wasn't my place to announce the prognosis or deliver any final news. Yet the woman was crying for a medical opinion and tightening her tortured grip on my hand hard enough that I wanted to tell her everything I knew.

"Will you pray with me, Chaplain? Pray that he will live!" For a moment I was stumped, knowing she was asking me to pray for an outcome that wasn't likely to happen. But then I realized that the miracle might not be in the outcome; it could come in the input. Prayer has the power to heal even when it doesn't cure. She was really asking me to pray for the healing of two lives—his and hers: his physical life and her life with him. So I prayed—hard. And at the moment of our "amen," the doctors emerged, stripping off their gloves and doing that solemn, cliché headshake they do.

The woman had popped out of her chair when they came

through the door, but she dropped back into it, sobbing, when she saw their verdict. I renewed my praying—this time for the eventual resurrection of that part of her that had just died. I prayed that God would begin the kind of miraculous healing that can't be measured with thermometers, EKGs, and blood pressure cuffs—the long, slow, grievous healing of a broken heart.

Knowing that healing can happen gives me hope. Knowing how it happens is outside my level of expertise. So if you asked me for help in understanding, I'd have to refer the question a little higher up.

THE BRAVEST WORDS

The only child of an aging couple, Brenda unknowingly faced the hardest moment of her life when she arrived at the hospital with her mother just minutes behind the ambulance carrying her father.

Brenda's mother was a stroke victim with moderate dementia, and John, Brenda's father, was his wife's caregiver. He drove her to all her appointments, paid the bills, did the shopping, and took care of the house. Busy with his care-giving duties, John had felt chest pains the entire day but had refused to seek help—until finally he collapsed, and a neighbor called 911. He came to the hospital breathing on his own, but he had waited too long. He was in trouble. Now drastic decisions needed to be made.

"Does he have a living will?" asked one of the ER staffers.

She was asking if he had a health-care advance directive, a document that tells the doctors, in advance, what you want done if you cannot speak for yourself. Without an advance directive, doctors are obligated to do "everything possible" to save your life—even if those life-saving measures only delay your death rather than prevent it.

Like a lot of people, John did not have one. But he was alert and declared that he wanted "everything possible" done to sustain his life.

In John's case, that meant he would need the support of a respirator. Indefinitely.

Respirators work well when doctors are expecting recovery, but John's heart was irreparably damaged, and the health team knew a respirator would only suspend him between life and death. As they huddled in the nurses' station, the charge nurse tapped the heart monitor screen. "Any minute now, this guy's going into cardiac arrest," she said. "What are we going to do, Doctor?"

His response voiced what all of them were thinking: "Nothing, I hope."

The nurses knew what they'd do if it was their loved one. They'd seen too many resuscitations to let their loved ones go that course. CPR is one of the most undignified of all procedures. Technicians rip open gowns and expose the whole of a person's physical being to a roomful of strangers. Nurses sometimes straddle the patient, placing their palms flat on the patient's chest, compressing the chest cavity in a rhythmic pulse. Ribs sometimes crack. The body sometimes expels waste. The procedure is done amazingly fast, and it may be repeated again and again until finally the patient cannot be resuscitated and is declared dead.

"Your father's heart is quite literally broken. The whole right side is dead," the doctor told Brenda. "We can't fix it. If we do 'everything,' he'll end up on a machine that will breathe for him, but he'll just keep having attacks. The way things stand now, your dad *will* have another heart attack, and we'll be obliged to perform endless CPR."

Hoping things wouldn't get that far, John's doctors asked Brenda to talk with her dad about changing his directive to them. In one of the bravest "talks" the staff had ever witnessed, she repeated the doctor's message with amazing clarity to her father.

"Dad, you know I love you, right?" she began. "I've always told you the truth. You taught me that. So I'm telling you the truth now, Dad. Your heart's broken."

"I know," he huffed. "Let's fix it and go home."

"Dad, listen to me," she pleaded while she stroked his hair. "They *can't* fix it, and if they try, you'll end up on a respirator for the rest of your life. I know you don't want that. Now you need to tell the doctor."

John looked at his wife, who was standing nearby, sadly repeating, "No, no, no."

Wrinkles swelled on his forehead. "Yes. They have to fix it," he argued. "Who will take care of mother?"

"Dad, they can't fix it. No one can," she said gently. "I'll take care of Mother. I promise."

"Will it hurt?" he asked.

The doctor, standing beside Brenda, promised, "We're going to make you comfortable, sir."

Brenda lowered her head, placing it gently on her father's chest. In a few moments, they exchanged words that couldn't be heard with human ears. And then came the words everyone heard: "OK," he said. "Let things happen as they happen."

For the remainder of the evening, the nurse administered comfort care only, and somewhere much later in the night, in a miraculous act of bravery, Brenda let her dad . . . let go.

THE LANGUAGE OF THE EYES

At our house we have rules about crying. Well, sort of. For instance, if my wife is crying at the end of the movie, the rest of us must pretend we don't notice. Otherwise, she cries more. I have two children who cry unabashedly by the bucketful and two other children who swear it's raining if they have a wet cheek. And me? Let's just say I wear a lot of sunglasses.

However, even the coolest shades couldn't hide the range of emotions flashing in my eyes one afternoon as another chaplain and I sat in our office at the hospital. When we heard a code blue call from the emergency room, we locked eyes. With only that look, a plethora of tragic scenarios were discussed between us in only a split second. We were also trying to determine which of us felt the most emotionally prepared to answer the call.

I stood up first.

In the ER, I was told to expect a family of Indian descent, a statement that caused me to wonder about being culturally prepared. I felt some uneasiness, anticipating the differences, and worried that my self-doubt would quickly become evident.

When the patient arrived, the ER staff moved very quickly into implementing a full response to her condition. Knowing the prognosis was grim, I took up my vigil in the ER waiting room, watching for the family's arrival but realizing I had forgotten their name. I was simply looking for an Indian family, a situation that felt like racial profiling for the most tragic reasons. But when the two young men hurried in, I needed no skin color to identify them; there was no need to look for different clothing or hair. The identifying mark was something I see in every family member I greet in the ER. It was something I could see in their eyes, a battle of terror and hope.

"Do you have our mother?" one of the men asked. "Can we see her?" The terror of possibilities was fighting against hope that would not give up ground. The battleground for the struggle being waged was in their eyes.

I ushered them into an adjoining family room, the room all families hope they'll never be taken. It is a place where hospitals hope to contain the family's explosion of grief, but for these two brothers, containment only brought a sense of being trapped. I could see panic starting to rise in their eyes.

When the doctor came into the room, they peppered him with questions. But without waiting for him to speak, they saw the answer in *his* eyes. Instantly, their tears welled, and their noses reddened. When the doctor confirmed their worst fears with a nod and a flatly dismissive sentence, disbelief exploded from within them.

It took them a few minutes to regain their composure, then they asked if they could see their mother. I took them to the room where she lay, and once again their sadness exploded into cries of disbelief and agony. Overhearing the noise, a security guard appeared. These days, any gathering of emotional people is subject to suspicion. Asking only with his eyes, the guard queried if I needed help. I shook my head no, but I noticed he still carried suspicion in his eyes.

As the guard left, more family members—the sisters and daughters—poured into the small room. Instantly a communication path opened, and the message of finality was conveyed— all from the sons' eyes to their family members.

The women streamed around the body and caressed every part of it. They held the woman's mouth as if to hush its pain, brushed her hair as if adjusting her crown, but most frequently, they stroked her eyelids as if to redirect her vision to another world. The room filled with a confusing cacophony of foreign words, but nothing was lost in the translation. The message was one of such abject grief it brought a trace of tears even to the eyes of a battle-hardened ER nurse. She tried to maintain a distant professionalism, but her eyes betrayed her emotional involvement.

Gradually, after some time, the tears and cries began to recede like the outgoing tide. Talk turned to funeral arrangements, and I could see that acceptance was gaining a brief toehold. The change was shown by their words but was most evident in their eyes.

I left the ER that day with a new understanding that grief is one of the great equalizers. Our skin color, culture, and religion may vary; political complexities may be difficult to understand. But the horrendous pain of losing a loved one is universal. If we can see that grief, I think we come closer to seeing the world through the eyes of God.

Part 4

MIRACLES IN UNIFORM

Hospital chaplains make a lot of difficult visits, but never have I witnessed such raw grief as I have on my visits to military homes these past few years while serving as chaplain with the Air National Guard.

This chapter is dedicated to our men and women in uniform and their families. Their service—and their sacrifice—are replete with miracles, both large and small.

THE DANCE

We've already established that the Bible says there's a time to weep and a time to laugh, a time to dance and a time to mourn (see Ecclesiastes 3:4). My problem is that every time I dance, people laugh; I suppose if I made an appearance on *American Idol*, the judges there might be moved to weep and mourn. Today I leave my denial and publicly acknowledge that I am "rhythmically challenged."

The deficit probably occurred due to my upbringing. My late father was a Baptist minister, and whenever I asked permission to attend a dance, he would pour on the guilt. Evidently he knew that songwriter George Michael was right: "guilty feet have got no rhythm."

The dancing ban continued through my college years at Baylor University, the biggest Baptist university in the world. Despite being lampooned by the late Christian comedian Grady Nutt, Baylor continued its no-dancing rule until 1994. Nutt used to quip that Baptists banned dancing because it enticed teenage couples to "go to the bushes." He said, "We weren't fools. We skipped the dancing and went straight to the bushes."

Since my college days, my head and heart have strived to move beyond the guilt of legalism, but when it comes to dancing, I have a split personality of sorts: Fred Astaire lives upstairs, but Jerry Falwell controls my feet.

Perhaps it's just as well. My inabilities to keep the beat have already become too well known, and not just in dancing. From

1999 to 2001, while I was on active duty at Patrick Air Force Base in Melbourne, Florida, the chapel staff became painfully aware that their chaplain had some rhythmic shortcomings, and they could be especially brutal about shielding the public from my deficiencies. Each Sunday, as I walked into the sanctuary early to consult with my music staff, Phil Black, the bandleader, would ask suspiciously, "What are you doing, Chaplain?"

I might say, with just a hint of suggestion in my voice, "I'm just wondering who's playing the congas today. You know, I've played percussion in worship before."

"Where?" Phil would ask suspiciously.

"In a Dallas temple once. It was run by a Hare Krishna group, and I had to go for an assignment in religion class at Baylor," I would proudly respond.

Acting in typical fashion, Phil would fire an order to the band: "Stow the percussion! Hide the incense! This man is dangerous."

I don't get any slack from my family either. As I stood at the front of the chapel during congregational singing, whenever the Spirit moved me I might start to sway a bit, getting into the vibrantly uplifting mood of the moment. Then, from the third pew, would come my wife's loving but firm sway of her head. *No*, she mouthed silently then added a pleading glance toward my teenage daughters, who were sinking off the pew in embarrassment.

At home, when an Elton John song awakens my enthusiastic (albeit misguided) moves, the kids run whining to their mother. "Mom! Mom!" they frantically cry. "He's dancing again. Make him stop! Please make him stop!"

Tragically, it looks like I'll never be able to heed the ecclesiastical call to dance—at least not in peace—but fortunately, I've been blessed to witness a good dance during a worship service.

It was performed by a talented girl named Brooke; she was a beautiful fourteen-year-old who loved to dance. I could never figure out why Phil didn't ask me to dance but would let Brooke perform anytime she wanted to. Well, yes, I could. Brooke didn't just dance; she inspired others to dance too.

When she was three weeks old, Brooke contracted spinal meningitis, which resulted in a condition called hydrocephalus— "water on the brain." The water causes the brain to swell, but with the help of a surgically implanted shunt, the water drains harmlessly into her gallbladder. As long as the shunt works, Brooke remains healthy, but occasionally it goes "on the fritz." Then her brain swells, and her dance—at least in this world—is threatened.

When she is healthy, Brooke dances with stunning beauty; she dances with great gratitude that she can dance at all. She dances as one who knows the music could stop and the dancing could end permanently. She dances with joy because she knows she has a devoted, adoring mother who would give her own life for the sake of her daughter.

Most of all, Brooke dances to celebrate the wonderfully close, personal relationship she has with God. As Brook choreographs a tangible demonstration of this relationship, she rises from the first pew and flows into the center aisle, gracefully gliding up and down as her willowy arms trace the letters of a love language enunciated through her sparkling eyes, fluttering fingers, and pointed toes.

When she first erupted in dancing, I was embarrassed, probably worried people would think our congregation was charismatic.

This dancing was not anywhere in the traditional Order of Worship!

My thinking was similar to that of a Pharisee Jesus mentioned. As the man sat on the front pew of the temple, he looked over his shoulder and saw a tax collector—a Roman collaborator, the most despised of all beings.

"Thank you, God, that I am not like thisssss man," he hissed.

And yet, Jesus would say that "this man," the hated tax collector, would be the one who was whole and "right with God" when he left the church. He added that the one who tried to exalt himself would find himself humbled, and the one who humbled himself would find himself exalted (see Luke 18:9–14).

Maybe that kind of humility is why Brooke can dance. In her dancing, Brooke never seems to exalt herself, but the One who fills her with so much joy she has to dance. Her love for God moves her feet in rhythm with an inner spirit.

Shortly before I left Patrick AFB, our world was knocked off its feet and slammed to the dance floor. Since 9/11 we, too, like Brooke, have had to face the threat that the music could stop and the dancing could end permanently. We have struggled to regain our rhythm and strained to hear the music. And we have found it playing in the hearts of people like Brooke who meet setbacks with determination and face the future with hope.

Pardon me, Brooke, but may I have this next dance?

THE SOLDIER'S GETHSEMANE MOMENT

There's a one-liner I often repeat: everyone yearns to go to heaven, but no one wants to be first in line to go there. Military life is much the same way—most are willing to serve, but few want to be first in line—especially a deployment line.

If you have ever wondered how soldiers miraculously find it within themselves to make that first step toward the front lines, come visit something called the Mobilization Processing Line. Early in Operation Enduring Freedom, I had the honor to watch twenty-five California Air National Guardsmen in my unit step into that line and answer the call to leave their homes and families and serve in the defense of our country.

Their journey began in the Mobilization Processing Line, a line of desks around the perimeter of a large room. Each desk was staffed by someone who would negotiate, confirm, provide, or approve each guardsman's details of deployment: immunizations, wills, dog tags, medical or dental issues, child-care arrangements, and personal problems.

Initially, the talk is light as guardsmen begin checking dog tags and trade punches on their freshly immunized arms. The beginning of the line also is full of good-natured complaints about the upcoming flights, the tight haircuts, or the size of their duffel bags. But further down the line, the questions and tasks become more serious. At a table labeled Dependent Care, a husband and wife, both about to be deployed, are questioned about their plan to leave their three children with friends.

At the legal table, someone's son signs a will leaving possessions to his mother. Another guardsman submits a power of attorney designating Dad as the one who will make health-care decisions if necessary.

Adjacent to that table, a female soldier verifies her only sister's address so the casualty notification teams can deliver the grim news that she is wounded, missing, or dead.

At the last table, I sit with the family support director and the squadron recruiter. The recruiter hands out pride items bearing squadron emblems—pencils, key rings, and calendars picturing a lot of fast jets. Moods lighten momentarily as soldiers grab the cool stuff and slap silly stickers on the back of an unsuspecting comrade.

The family support table is loaded with coloring books depicting Major Mom walking a Jetway lined with flag-waving well-wishers. The support director demonstrates the new videophones for two moms eager to call home; in turn, the moms show off pictures of newborns. Beside them, another soldier asks someone to check on his pregnant wife.

As they come to me, I hand them a camouflage Bible and joke about listing the soldiers' sins on their deployment approval sheet. All jokes aside, they know I'm the last guy who might be able to detour them from their mandatory destination. It is here that eyes moisten and faces harden as I ask, "Soldier, is there anything that would prevent you from going on this deployment?"

I ask the question because not everyone snaps a proverbial salute at the receipt of his or her orders. It's possible that some are feeling a conscientious objection to our country's latest action. Others may feel depressed, even to the point that they worry they may in some way be a danger to themselves or others.

Others may have hoped to retire soon or to just get out, but the military says they perform such an essential job, they can't leave unless death do them part. It's a predicament the military calls a stop/loss order, and usually it brings the same excitement a draft notice might bring an eighteen-year-old.

All such possibilities aside, 99 percent are ready to go. They have prepared themselves, recognizing fate or predestination or some larger force outside themselves that has helped them reach this point. But despite their philosophizing, there is still a lot of struggling going on beneath their commitment-camou-flaged exterior. As they leave families, homes, and jobs, their psyche is a mixing bowl swirling with fear, pride, and bravado.

Each year Christians honor a moment in which Jesus also found himself struggling with something he had to do. The struggle took place in the Garden of Gethsemane where, hoping God might spare him from impending crucifixion, Jesus prayed, "If it be possible, let this cup pass from me" (Matthew 26:39 KJV).

For these troops, their time in the Mobilization Processing Line was their "Gethsemane moment." Here they got a taste of the cup they would have to drink; here they confirmed that they would do the job our leaders were sending them to do, whether or not they agreed with its merit.

For most of them, their willingness to drink "this cup" would harden their resolve to win the fight and come home to those they love.

A DELAY OF SACRED REMEMBRANCE

Last year, after sitting in a weeklong conference for National Guard chaplains, I boarded a plane for my return trip from Baltimore. The conference had been especially long, and as a guy whose wife believes that God called him to preach because he can't sit still in a pew, I was more than anxious to see my family and sleep in my own bed.

I wasn't the only military person on the plane who was eager to get home. Baltimore-Washington International is the connecting airport for military troops returning from the war zone, and a group of soldiers were filing onto the plane. As we were buckling seat belts, the baggage carts that were just then pulling up alongside the plane meant our homecoming would be delayed.

Using the plane's PA system, the pilot solicited our sympathies, explaining that we would wait for the soldiers' bags to be loaded. "It's bad enough that they've been over there risking their lives," he explained. "I'm not letting them go home without their luggage."

Inspired by the pilot's announcement, the passengers readily agreed. "It's the least we could do," reasoned the woman seated across from me.

"Ba, ba, ba," noted another passenger, not yet teething.

"Everything happens for a reason," philosophized a third passenger.

As the soldiers boarded, I searched their faces, and my mind flashed back to the events of a month prior. I wondered if one particular face was missing. It was the face of Sergeant Joseph Torres— a face I only knew by the pictures on his mother's coffee table.

Summer had come early that warm day when we knocked on the door of Christina Torres to tell her that her son, Joseph, was not coming home. As she opened the door, she forestalled the announcement she must have known was coming from the two men in dress military uniforms. She offered us iced tea and invited us to sit down on the comfortable couch. I was confident her gracious greeting had all the respect Joseph had shown his fellow soldiers—the kind of respect he'd been taught by this military family.

But we had not come for a social visit, and no offer of refreshments could take away the awful words we brought with us. My colleague had memorized them on the hour-long ride to her home. When she offered him a seat, the sergeant solemnly replied, "I'd rather stand, ma'am."

Mrs. Torres stood too.

Then the sergeant took a breath and rattled off his memorized soliloquy: "The secretary of the army," he said in a voice seemingly impervious to the tears forming in his eyes, "regrets to inform you that your son, Sergeant Joseph Torres was killed May 24, 2004."

Suddenly his speech hit a snag, and for a brief second the sergeant's words were caught by the lump in his throat. Then he took another breath and continued with the devastating news: Sergeant Torres, twenty-four, had died in Baghdad when the vehicle in which he was riding overturned as the driver swerved to avoid another vehicle.

Having stood longer than I'd have thought possible, Mrs. Torres finally broke our little formation and dropped back onto the overstuffed couch. The sergeant and I eased into the two chairs facing her, and over the next hour we huddled to hear the stories and admire the pictures of Joseph's childhood.

It was those pictures that had brought to mind Joseph's face as I watched the soldiers file onto what might have been, for all I knew, the flight Joseph had planned to take for a surprise homecoming that month.

"Ladies and gentlemen, it looks like we're ready to go." The pilot's voice interrupted my melancholic haze. "Flight attendants, if you'll prepare the cabin for departure, we'll be pushing off from the gate momentarily."

At home the next day, I read news accounts of some airline flights that had been delayed the day before, not by late-arriving bags, but by a computer glitch. In my business, however, I don't put much stock in glitches or coincidences. I much prefer the term "God moments."

Yesterday's "God moment" had been, for me, nothing short of a miracle. Rather than a delay for baggage loading, it had been a delay of sacred remembrance—remembrance that people like Sergeant Torres would not be counted as simply another casualty in the total for the week but as a real person, one who was willing to put his life on the line, risking a celestial homecoming instead of an earthly one. And in this exchange, he and others like him guarantee that the rest of us will continue to have places we eagerly return to. Places we call home.

SO YOU THINK YOU'RE A STUD!

During my days of service as an air force chaplain, I enjoyed a lot of titles. Navy folks called me Chappy. British colleagues called me Padre. A Vietnam vet even used to call me Sky Pilot after the 1968 Eric Burdon song. However, none of those names compare to what I was once called at our hospital's senior center. As I walked into the center one afternoon, the recreation director spotted me and keyed the microphone to make her usual announcement: "We are now ready for our Bible study." But this time, a slip of the tongue caused a slight variation in her last word, and she inadvertently prepped this audience of one hundred seniors for the arrival of the "Bible stud."

Studs are usually tough guys, and while everyone was playfully amused with my new title, they knew I wasn't all that tough. Few of us guys are the tough studs we imagine ourselves to be. Toughness can be a costume we don to hide our need to be somebody we're not. At one time or another, we've all put on

the tough-guy act—or met someone auditioning for the part.
Late one night I met one such tough guy I'll never forget.

The meeting took place on a darkened street just outside the
chapel where I was serving as an active duty chaplain in Turkey.
The players involved in this little scene included myself, an army
sergeant, and his wife and children.

As I left the chapel that night I heard, from just beyond the edge
of the streetlights, a woman demanding to be released. Then came
a man's answer, a reply so harsh it would have caused some to
blush. Instead it caused *me* to flush—with anger. Evidently this
tough guy was one of those men who thought being a stud meant
making a woman "do what you're told."

Imagining myself to be a bit of a stud, I hurried toward the
sound of the confrontation and found myself standing toe-to-
toe with an army sergeant. In the melodramatic style of an old
Dragnet episode, I initiated an introduction: "I'm Chaplain
Burkes," I asserted, offering my ID. "May I see your ID please?"

In the next few moments we mutually examined each other's
ID like we were putting poker hands on a table. The sergeant had
no choice but to fold, considering my better hand as a captain.

"Let her go, Sergeant!" I told him.

He let her go but grabbed the children in trade. "She can go,"
he answered angrily, "but the children go with me!"

"Let them go, Sergeant!" I said in my best tough-guy staccato. Seeing him hesitate, I ratcheted up the command a notch:
"That's an order!" I barked. "A direct order!"

Now, if your military knowledge is limited to old reruns of
Hogan's Heroes, you might think captains are always barking,
"That's an order!" But actually it's very rare. In fact, in my
twenty years as a military chaplain, this was the only time I ever

said it, but it worked. He released his hold on the kids. I told him I would escort his wife and children home, and I directed him to separate quarters.

"Sergeant, you will report to my office by noon tomorrow," I told him. "If you don't show up, I'll bring this incident to your commander's office. If you do show up, I can promise you complete confidentiality in our counseling." This promise followed military guidelines that give every person I counseled complete confidentiality. Even if someone were to confess a murder or a treasonous act, as chaplain I could not reveal that to anybody. But, like any other officer, if I personally observed a wrongful act—as I had done that night—I could report it to his commander.

He knew that, which was probably why he showed up for the appointment the next day. Emboldened by the confidential sanctuary of the chaplain's office, the sergeant and his wife came in, and both screamed at and threatened each other with divorce and child-custody battles. Things quickly became so venomous that future counseling appointments were scheduled separately.

Over the next several days, however, the husband finally began talking about what toughness had meant with his "old man" and about the toughness the army had taught him, a characteristic he had transferred to his home life. After many hours of talk and introspection, this tough-guy stud finally broke down and admitted he wasn't so tough after all. He spoke of dark times sitting in his fifth-floor apartment window night after night, wanting to jump, and he described a presence that held him in that window and would not let him do it. He talked of his failing family life and his career. He told me his family needed a miracle.

"Is there any hope?" he asked.

I told him it all depended on his willingness to redefine and

transform what it meant to be a tough stud. He said he was willing, and he quickly set about proving the truth of his words.
Eventually, the husband and wife began to rebuild their love for
each other and for their Creator. They took classes in anger management and sought the support of a faith community. They
pledged a new commitment to the biblical admonition to submit
themselves "one to another in the fear of God" (Ephesians 5:21
KJV). Not her submitting to him, as he had demanded that she
do, but choosing to submit equally to each other in love.

Sometime later that year, as I prepared for my return to the
United States, I looked them up to say my good-byes. "Chaplain,"
she said, "when you look at us now, you'd have to say you were
looking at a miracle."

I smiled at the understatement. Then I noticed another miracle. She must have caught the question in my eyes.

"Yup, I'm pregnant," she said, beaming.

"And I made promotion," he added as the miracles continued.

Besides the biological meaning of *stud*, the dictionary gives
another meaning: "a strengthening crosspiece." That's the kind
of stud the sergeant became the day he wept before his wife and
his Creator in search of forgiveness. A miracle had happened: by
admitting his weakness he had become the stud—the strengthening crosspiece—of a new relationship.

Using this definition, maybe I can be a stud after all.

THE DREADED KNOCK ON THE DOOR

Military chaplains are quick to recognize the phone number of
Mortuary Affairs when it appears on their pagers. Messages from
this office usually summon the death notification team to carry the
tragic news to someone that he or she has lost a family member.

One Saturday afternoon, I was mowing the front yard of our home on an air force base when my wife emerged from our house waving my pager over her head. A chorus of pagers had beeped the sour note all over the base, summoning our four-person team (a commander, a paralegal, a medic, and myself) to perform the dreaded duty.

When we arrived at the Mortuary Affairs office, it was obvious that the support personnel had already choreographed our parts. After a quick briefing, we were given maps and the keys to a government sedan. Next to the keys was a packet of family information on the deceased: names, legal documents, and death-benefit brochures. On top of the packet was a training video demonstrating the particulars of death notification. Popping the video into the VCR, we sat back to watch a vignette that tempted us with an illusion of predictability.

"Are you Mrs. Jim E. Smith?" asked the actor playing the part of the commander.

"Yes."

"Is your husband Sgt. Jim E. Smith? Social Security number 555-55-5555?"

"Yes. What's this all about?"

"May we come in?" was the scripted reply.

Once inside, the commander delivered his line, a somber cliché: "Ma'am, we regret to inform you that your husband, Sgt. Jim E. Smith, was killed today while in the service of our country."

Actual notifications, however, rarely go as scripted in the video portrayal. As the video's credits rolled, the Mortuary Affairs chief explained the particulars of our impending visit.

"The major died while overseas on temporary duty, and he leaves a wife and two kids in base housing," he said in a professional tone. Then he added, "Please be aware that a cadre of four officers in dress uniform is going to alarm anyone living in base housing."

He was right. As we drove through the housing area of the large air base, kids held their basketballs, lawnmowers veered off their paths, and screen doors slammed behind those coming out to see where our car would stop.

"That's it," the medic said, pointing to a house while keeping his finger on the map. We stopped, stared, and held our breath. Balloons bobbed on the mailbox, and a Happy Birthday sign was posted on the lawn.

The commander rustled through her file, releasing a sigh and a whispered swear word. "Here's a little detail someone missed," she said. "One of the kids has a birthday today."

"Can't we come back tomorrow?" the medic asked.

"You want the kid learning about his dad on CNN?" retorted the commander. She jerked the car's door handle, and the rest of us rolled out then followed her up the sidewalk in sync with her step. We paused on the front porch, and she rang the doorbell.

"I don't know what this is all about," said the woman answering the door, "but whatever it is, it'll need to wait until after the birthday party." She knew what it was about, of course. And, no, it couldn't wait.

"Are you Mrs. Smith?" the commander asked.

The woman answered by silently motioning us into a private room, where the commander finished her script and the medic watched for signs of fainting. At the wife's request, I read a passage of Scripture and prayed. The paralegal explained how her husband's body would be escorted home by a trusted friend.

As family members and friends arrived for the party, some took over our consoling role while others turned away party-goers, whispering the unspeakable news. After a while we left the woman and her family in the care of their friends and their church. But although we left the house, we couldn't leave behind the events of the day, which stayed in our minds and rattled our emotions.

For you see, we had just performed a real-life scene—a real-life nightmare—that is often rehearsed in the mind of every service member and anyone related to a service member. We left the house knowing, *Someday this could happen at my house.* We grieved with that woman and her children knowing, *Someday this could be my spouse and family.*

Military families know these terrifying possibilities could happen to them. Yet every day, spouses, friends, children, and parents unwrap their arms from their brave loved ones and watch as they walk away, down airport jetways, heading into harm's way. These families know that, even as they pray for their loved ones' safe return, some of them will receive instead the dreaded knock at the door.

In honor of those families, and in memory of our nation's fallen heroes, I ask that you pause with me a moment to admire the miraculous and unwavering tenacity of those who've stormed sandy beaches, braved steaming jungles, and endured scalding desert heat to serve their country—and also the devoted loyalty of those who have waited anxiously back home. In this moment of remembrance, let's say thank you to all those families. And may all our prayers anticipate a day when we can beat our swords into plowshares and no one has to hear a uniformed officer say the dreaded words, "We regret to inform you . . ."

PROMOTION ON A DIFFERENT LEVEL

As a military chaplain, promotion ceremonies usually mean I'm called upon to wear my best uniform and voice a formal prayer. To be honest, these ceremonies are pretty routine (some would even say boring) for everyone except the one being promoted and his or her family members. The programs roll through a litany of military traditions that make them indistinguishable from one another to those who are merely onlookers.

Yet one promotion ceremony stands out in my memory from the dozens of such events I've witnessed. It was the promotion of Lt. Cmdr. Alan Tubbs, which took place in the hospital where I worked as chaplain. I will never forget that day.

A young man—a boy, actually—lay in the hospital bed. This was Alex, mentioned earlier in the story "One More Breath." On this day, Alex's mother enveloped his cadaverous face in her hands and summoned him from his cancer drug–induced slumber. "Alex," she said, "wake up. Look who's here."

Alex opened his eyes to find his hospital bed surrounded by several people, including a trio of men wearing the dress white uniform of the United States Coast Guard. The audience was comprised of his parents, his dad's commander, a Coast Guard chaplain, a few nurses, and myself.

"Alex," his mom said, "your dad is being promoted today. Right now!"

Realizing he was the guest of honor, Alex pushed his chapped lips into a wide, proud smile.

In the call-up of reservists after 9/11, Alan Tubbs had answered the call. And judging by the amazing collection of military paraphernalia that decorated Alex's room, the son was awfully proud of his father.

Alan's commander, or Skipper, as he was called, began the ceremony by announcing he had a promotion order that came from the president of the United States, "acting upon the recommendation of the secretary of the navy." The Skipper told us the president had "placed special trust and confidence" in Alex's dad because he had shown "special qualities and demonstrated potential to serve in the higher grade."

Tradition allows a family member to pin on the new emblem signifying a change in rank, and when it was time, Alex's dad leaned over the hospital bed to offer Alex his epaulet. "Alex, can you unbutton the epaulet for me, buddy?" he asked tenderly.

Confused by all his medications, Alex fumbled with his breathing tubes.

"No, no, Alex, not that," his dad corrected. "My shirt— unbutton my shirt."

"Oh," Alex exhaled with a sense of embarrassment, unbuttoned the epaulet, and slid on the new rank. When his dad straightened up again, the room burst into happy applause.

With the official ceremony ended, the Skipper pulled out a different paper and began a second, more personal, ceremony. As the military members stood at attention, he humbly read the words of the certificate that expressed the gratitude that he and the United States Coast Guard held for Alex.

"Your father was required to do Coast Guard work that prevented him from spending more time with you," the Skipper read. "He would have preferred to be home to help you when you needed him, but his outstanding work in support of our country was also very important to your future. The United States Coast Guard thanks you, Alex, for your support."

Everyone applauded again, and this time everyone also

cried. As I had listened to all the words of the two ceremonies, I became aware that this was a miraculous gathering of mutual encouragers. Alex and his mother had encouraged Alex's dad. And now his dad and all the others in the gathering, along with godparents and church members outside the hospital, were encouraging Alex to run a strong race for life. They were people who had encouraged him when he wavered in his fight against the cancer, prayed for him when he was weak, and urged him to keep running the race.

A few months later, another change occurred, and we saw Alex miraculously promoted to a higher and more spiritual rank. On that day we tearfully watched him cross the finish line. As his breathing labored, his mother placed her hand on his face, and they were connected again. Alex suddenly flashed us all a smile, and then he breathed his last breath.

Watching him, I was suddenly blessed with an image of his arrival in heaven. Then a Scripture from Hebrews came to mind: "Therefore, since we are surrounded by such a huge crowd of witnesses to the life of faith, let us strip off every weight that slows us down, especially the sin that so easily hinders our progress. And let us run with endurance the race that God has set before us" (12:1 NLT).

The "race" God had set before Alex had ended, and he had been promoted to heavenly status. I imagined the angelic witnesses cheering him on as he crossed the finish line, calling, "Well done, Alex. Welcome home!"

Part 5

MIRACLES ON THE HOME FRONT: THE PERSONAL LIFE OF A CHAPLAIN

Many people may believe chaplains have a challenging career while enjoying a spiritual life that's free of doubts and questions. These are probably the same people who think chaplains' homes are always harmonious and nurturing settings where voices are never raised in anger, doors are never slammed in frustration, kids never misbehave, and parents never go bonkers. Oh, and also where house pets never have accidents.

In case this is your mental image of a chaplain's personal life, I'm including this selection of stories to set you straight. My family and I are living proof that pastoral people are as human as anyone else. Like most humans, I have emotional hot buttons—and I have a wife and kids who know how to push them. I've been known to hit *their* temperamental trip wires occasionally myself. I have fears and worries, I tend to be set in my ways, and I know the inside of an emergency room not only as a hospital professional but also as a worried parent.

In this last chapter, I'd like to invite you into my life and my home so you can get an inside look at the personal side of a chaplain. Come on in. Don't mind the mess.

"I TAKE THEE, NORRIS"

During my adolescent years I seemed to have a lot of trouble pronouncing my name with any sort of confident clarity. Absent the self-assured inflection I'd heard in the voice of my mentors, my pronunciation often communicated more self-doubts than any kind of identity. When I tried telling people, "My name is Norris," the resulting confusion caused many to respond with a monosyllabic question: "What?"

Repeating my name for them only seemed to frustrate my inquisitors. "Did you say *Morris*?" Or they'd ask, "Yes, but what's your first name?"

By 1975, I'd had enough of the confusion. When I was offered a summer church-camp job at Glorieta Baptist Assembly Grounds in Glorieta, New Mexico, a thousand miles from my home, I saw an opportunity to audition a name change. I entered the gates of the conference grounds in June 1975 practiced and ready so that when the first person asked my name, I could blurt it out without hesitation. "Hi, I'm Ed," I said pleasantly. I'd not only changed to my middle name, but I was already using its abbreviated version.

Out in the middle of New Mexico's high desert, the name-change experiment seemed harmless enough. After all, it was only a summer job.

I still remember that first person's reply: "What? Did you say *Fred*?"

It was quickly obvious that my wealth of pleasantry didn't make up for my lack of confidence; apparently I was still mum-

123

bling my name. *Ed* seemed to have left my mouth with no more clarity than had *Norris*.

Within days of finishing my summer job—and with a lot of encouragement from my mother, who reminded me that she wouldn't have named me *Norris* if she had intended for me to go by *Ed*—I returned to Norris. So as I headed for Baylor University in Texas that fall, I figured I would shed the Ed and become Norris once more.

Not so fast. I wasn't the camp's only staff member headed for Baylor. Imagine the surprise of the freshman girl I escorted to the homecoming bonfire when I was greeted by two other girls calling me Ed. In the dorm, other New Mexico friends continually introduced me as Ed, compounding the confusion to those who I'd introduced myself to as Norris. I had to repeatedly remind my roommates not to discard any mail addressed to Ed Burkes.

By my sophomore year, David Allan Coe's song "You Never Even Call Me by My Name" became a favorite song of mine. But by my senior year, I'd persuaded all my friends to call me Norris once again—with only one exception. That exception came from an especially spunky blonde I'd met in that New Mexico camp. And through all four years of college, my roommates would often return from the mailbox with one of her letters. "Yoo-hoo, oh Ed!" they'd call, mimicking her with a falsetto voice. "She wrote you another letter."

It took a lot of persuasion to get this girl, Becky, to call me Norris. She preferred the name Ed, and it seemed as though she'd never concede. But finally, on January 4, 1980, she finally made a pledge to forever call me Norris.

"I take thee, Norris, to be my wedded husband," she said that day. "To have and to hold from this day forward, for richer or poorer, in sickness and in health, 'til death do us part."

Note to my sweetheart on the year of our twenty-sixth anniversary: You've always known who I am—even though I often lack a clue. Your love changes me because it honors the best in me. It is a love for the person God created me to be—not what I should be or could be or would have been. In that love, I find the most cherished reminder of the love of God. And that is something that both Ed and Norris will cherish forever.

DON'T ASK MY WIFE TO PRAY FOR YOU!

Unless you're really serious, I wouldn't suggest that you ask my wife to pray for you. Trust me. Becky's got a reputation for her prayers; the fact is, sometimes they hurt.

A few years back, she decided to pray for Sara, our college-student daughter who was so so heavily involved in college busyness that we could rarely get her to answer her cell phone. My wife's prayer was that Sara would find a way to get more rest.

A week later, Sara broke her thumb and had to drop several extracurricular activities.

Apparently the prayer was a doozy, because this wasn't your everyday broken thumb. It was a break that required her to fly home from school, find a specialist, and have surgery.

About that same time, Becky prayed to find more quality time to spend with our twelve-year-old daughter, Nicole. The day after Sara returned to school when she had recovered from thumb surgery, Nicole broke her foot. The doctor prescribed no walking, and Nicole spent many hours with my wife over the next two months. Prayer granted.

Then Becky turned her prayers loose on me. Like Sara, I,

too, had been keeping a hectic schedule, and Becky prayed that I'd slow my writing schedule so I could spend more quality time with my family. Her prayer locked on to me sometime Saturday afternoon as I finished one writing project and was assembling my entry for a writing contest while also working on a sermon I had promised to preach for our pastor and making cross-country travel arrangements to receive an award I had won.

Suddenly, in the midst of all this multitasking, I grabbed my chest. It hurt to breathe, and the pain stretched from my navel to my throat. I wanted to think *heartburn* and feel confident I'd be OK. But as a hospital chaplain, I've heard too many people sing the heartburn tune of denial only to have it quickly become their funeral dirge. So, with the calm demeanor of a drowning rat, I asked Becky to take me to the emergency room. Within a few minutes of my arrival, I was given my first nitroglycerin tablet.

Nitro tablets are what the ER staff gives middle-aged men who are suffering angst about their health. It gives you a nice headache, which helps you forget about your chest pain. Well, the short version of this story is that I stayed twenty-three hours for observation and was released the following day.

Diagnosis: heartburn from hell.

Person to blame (at least in my opinion): my loving wife and her prayers.

Lesson learned: when you're married to a prayer warrior, you *will* end up doing the right thing, one way or the other!

Becky's prayer hit its mark with accurate precision; it hadn't been intended as a fatal blow to my extracurricular writing activities. It was merely a warning shot over my bow, or perhaps more accurately, it was intended only to wing me. That's exactly what happened. My busy schedule slowed significantly, and Becky put another notch in her prayer belt.

I've told you already that I met Becky at a church camp in New Mexico during the summer before I started college. But my prayers to find her actually began many years earlier in a junior high boys' camp when my camp counselor shared his secret for finding the most wonderfully caring and stunningly gorgeous woman in the world. Of course, all we cared about back then were the stunning and gorgeous parts, but we listened anyway as he opened his Bible and read a passage from Matthew: "Seek first [God's] kingdom and his righteousness, and all these things will be given to you as well" (6:33).

We stared at him blankly. Then one of my tentmates expelled an unbelieving grunt, prompting the counselor to explain: "If you follow that advice," he said, "it won't matter what the woman looks like to anyone else. To you, she'll be stunningly gorgeous."

With that anticlimactic remark, he slammed shut his Bible and turned off the light.

His words had an unexpected effect on me. As I lay there looking at the ceiling of our tent, I was suddenly certain of two things: I wanted to be a minister, and I wanted a really fine girl. (And, like most boys my age, the majority of my attention was on the latter.) Those were the things I prayed for that night . . . and for many nights after.

Despite my typically skewed adolescent priorities, ten years later God gave me "a really fine girl." Knowing what I know now, I'm sure our meeting came about more as a result of her prayers than from my own prayerful requests that began with the testosterone-charged plea that night at camp. Now, after twenty-six years of marriage, she continues to pray for me, continually asking God to help me keep my priorities straight by seeking his will for my life.

Her prayers sometimes take a circuitous route, and yes, sometimes people have been slightly injured in the process, but everyone's OK in the end. So lately I've been thinking of posting a prayer-request list on my Web site, offering to ask Becky to pray for those who sign up. But I warn you: don't ask her unless you're serious. And don't be surprised if I ask you to sign a release form first!

A SON'S TUMBLE, A FATHER'S TEARS

At fifteen years old, my son became one of the fifty thousand kids served annually by emergency room physicians treating skateboard accidents.

OK, I know what you're thinking: *Chaplain, don't you spend enough time in emergency rooms to know that you shouldn't let your kids have skateboards?*

Well, you see, that's the thing. I didn't actually give him the skateboard. That would violate the agreement I have with my wife: no skateboards for him and no skydiving for me. This was a skateboard he borrowed just to take it for a spill—er, I mean spin.

The whole thing happened within an hour of our family's safe return from vacation. Our prayers for "traveling mercies," as we call them in our tradition, had been answered. But I guess we should have added a skateboard extension. I don't know why we neglected that part. It's not like extra prayers cost extra or anything.

Anyway my son was apparently so happy to be home with

his friends that he immediately took off and went skateboarding with them after dark. You might say he encountered unexpected turbulence as a car whizzed past him, and he went down, kissing the pavement. He arose with a bleeding chin; his friends thoughtfully provided a towel before he turned his direction toward home.

Arriving on our front porch, he flung open the door and announced, "I'm giving up skateboarding." (I admire his decisiveness about giving up something he's not allowed to do.) "Don't worry," he added. "My best friend did the same thing, and he didn't have to have stitches."

Stitches? Stitches! I hadn't even been thinking about the possibility of stitches.

"Let me take a look," his mother said, pulling back the towel. (I see hospital blood all day long, but when it belongs to my kid, I do the smart thing: I let their mother look.)

"Norris! You need to look at this," she called.

Yup, there it was—a gaping hole in his chin. "I think that's what they call a 'puncture wound,'" was my amateur diagnosis. It was about the size of an eraser, and it got darker as it went deeper. "ER trip!" I announced.

But while I was examining the hole, his mother noticed something altogether different. It was something I hadn't even thought of looking for. I mean, this boy was fifteen at the time! But there it was: a glistening in his eyes that was producing just enough liquid to spawn a tear. Then, as quickly as it appeared, it disappeared into the dirt on his face. His mother looked at me as if to say, *OK, Chaplain, tears are your department.*

So, remembering his fifteen-year-old pride, I gently perched him on the edge of my knees—all on the pretense of taking a closer look. And for a moment, I did just that: looked at him. It was as if I had just watched the last bit of childhood innocence and hurt escape right in front of me. For, at his age, many young men have already dug a pretty deep place where they hope to stow those tears for the duration of manhood.

But my hope for him is that it will only be a place where his feelings hibernate—and don't petrify. A place where they stay only long enough to develop and transform into tears that become a reflecting pool of his authenticity. From his perch on my knee, he allowed me a quick hug and a reassuring hand through his hair. "Yup, it looks like you'll need stitches," I said.

Later, when we had returned from the emergency room, his mother asked, "Did it hurt?"

"Nah," he said as he bolted out to show his friends his new battle scars.

"Well," I said adding a postscript to his answer, "at least not for *him*."

CAST YOUR VOTE

As someone who has been raised as a Baptist, I can tell you not much happens in Baptist churches without a vote. We don't change carpet, staff, or even our underwear without a vote. (OK, just kidding about the underwear. But seriously, Baptists love to vote.)

In the 1960s, I attended a Southern Baptist church in Berkeley, California. It was a time when antiwar groups protesting the Vietnam War were taking over churches to stage sit-ins. Our church spent hours discussing what we might do if our pulpit were hijacked. And then we voted, and the vote was unanimous. If our church were commandeered by campus radicals, the members resolved to quietly rise and march around the church singing, "We Shall Overcome."

My father-in-law, a Baptist pastor during those turbulent sixties, told me of one vote he always dreaded. Every time Christmas came on a Sunday, the congregation would vote on whether to hold the regularly scheduled evening worship service.

With Sunday night worship a Baptist tradition since the invention of the light bulb, the vote was almost always in favor of having the service. My father-in-law didn't mind upholding the Baptist tradition, but he hated to be the only one who actually showed up. One year, he devised a plan. "All in favor *and who will be in attendance*, indicate by the uplifting of your right hand," he said.

With only a hand or two reluctantly raised, he offered the alternative choice: "All opposed and who elect to worship at home with their families, indicate by the uplifting of your right hand."

That was the year "home worship" won out.

Every year on the anniversary of the Supreme Court's *Roe v. Wade* decision, another vote, of sorts, is scheduled. It's the annual vote against abortion. In hundreds of cities across the United States and Canada demonstrators carry signs that proclaim, Abortion Kills Children, Adoption Is a Loving Option, and Jesus Forgives and Heals.

The signs express strong opinions, but, especially as I think about urging adoption as a loving option, I can't help wondering how many of the demonstrators are like the church members who voted to hold Sunday night service without obliging to attend. I can't help wondering how many of them move on to the next level of commitment and follow through with their adoption advocacy.

Several years ago, my wife and I were locked in a tie vote, one to one. Our debate began as pictures of a blonde-haired, blue-eyed, two-year-old girl spilled out of an envelope and onto our kitchen table. The pictures were from the foster parents of our first two adopted children. The parents were giving us unofficial notice that our children had a sister and our family would soon have another adoption option.

We faced a choice—a vote. "Looks like we're going to have another child," I told my wife.

"I'm not sure we can do that," she answered.

"Do we have a choice?" I asked in a tone that betrayed my feelings.

The crisis we were facing felt similar to what a woman must feel when she finds herself with an accidental pregnancy. We argued with God, with each other, and with anyone else who would listen. A family of five (our biological daughter plus a son and daughter by adoption) was big enough, Becky worried. How could we manage with six? We already struggled with many issues similar to those experienced by blended families. How could we find the patience for so many children? Neither our car nor our military quarters seemed big enough. And we also worried, *Can our hearts really be big enough?*

I asked my wife if we could "table the motion" and asked the social worker to schedule a visit for us with the little girl. It was a dirty trick, but my wife knows I'm pretty good at parliamentary procedures. Like I said, I'm a Baptist. After the visit, there was no longer a need to vote. The little girl joined her biological siblings and became facetiously known to her new parents as "our little accident."

It was a great day, and not just because it meant getting a new SUV the size of a small school bus. It was a great day because God was giving us an opportunity to not just voice an opinion but to demonstrate our commitment through our actions.

Voicing an opinion is easy. Making a commitment is not. People on both sides of the abortion argument have reasons to commit to adoption; as I write this, newspaper stories report that 488 foster children are missing in Los Angeles County alone. Missing! Lost in the system. Or maybe just lost. The sobering number shows how great the need is for both sides to work on creating a system where mothers see unwanted pregnancies develop into wanted children. As we all begin to look for ways to care for the children who are already here, we create an environment where mothers can choose to bring babies into the world knowing there are full ranges of loving adoption choices.

Whether you're pro-life or pro-choice, adoption is the strongest statement you can make to support your position. The corroborating scriptural teaching is, "Faith without works is dead" (James 2:20, 26 KJV). The corroborating platitudes could be, Put your money where your mouth is, or, Put up or shut up.

Jesus scolded his disciples one day because they kept the noisy children away from him. He told them not to prevent the children from coming to him because theirs would be the kind of spirits that would comprise the kingdom of God.

As I watch demonstrators march along both sides of the abortion line, I have to ask, Has the debate become so noisy that we have drowned out the cries of those who have already been born and are waiting for people of faith to cast their vote for adoption?

MY WORLD, TURNED UPSIDE DOWN

The SUV I bought for my growing family safely carried us for ten years until one day last year, when it was called upon to give itself up for my daughter. You might say it was the day my world was turned upside down. Well, not literally my world. More precisely, it was the SUV that turned upside down. And it wasn't so much that the SUV was upside down on a dirt road as it was that my daughter was inside the SUV, hanging upside down from her seatbelt.

Yes, she was fine—everyone was fine. Well, maybe not everyone. Dad's wallet suffered some sprains and contusions. You see, I wasn't carrying collision insurance, and the SUV was totaled. With the cost of insuring three teenagers, I'd dropped the expensive collision coverage in favor of eating three meals a day. It was an attempt to balance the risk between paying exorbitant premiums and possibly paying out-of-pocket to replace our older vehicle.

The insurance agent had warned me about the risk of dropping the coverage. She urged caution, saying the car still had a lot of life left in it. Of course it did, and it gave that life to save my daughter, for which I am eternally grateful. No, I'm not mad at the SUV. If there's anything—or anyone—I want to kick right now, it's me.

What was I thinking?

I'll tell you what I was thinking, although as I look at the crumpled SUV, I admit it sounds a little lame right now. Insurance agents and appliance salespeople like to scare you with that word *risk*, as in, "Do you want to risk not buying an extended warranty for that washing machine, Mrs. Burkes?"

To which I reply, "Hey, she married me, didn't she? An extended warranty isn't even in her vocabulary!"

But this whole dirt-road, high-adrenaline experience has caused me to think more about our society's relationship with risk. The fact is, most of us don't like taking risks. We want to insure it, protect it, manage it, cure it, readjust it, reposition it, balance it, deny it, and, in some cases, prevent it. Risk shines a light on our vulnerabilities, and like a molting crustacean, we want to hide under a rock when we're vulnerable and be protected from whatever is out there. The biggest risk we'll ever take isn't deciding whether to drop collision insurance on an aged SUV. The biggest risk is loving someone, because love freely given comes with no guarantees; the people we love are under no obligation to return that love. In loving my child—or anyone, for that matter—I have to take risks. I have to put my heart on the line—with no collision insurance—and trust God will conspire to keep us safe so neither of us ends up totaled on a dirt road.

Jesus knew something about the risk of relationships. He risked everything to disciple a group of anglers. Perhaps Jesus was teaching us how futile it is to try to get insurance on love. After all, he asked Peter three times, "Do you love me?"

And Peter replied each time, "You know it."

Yet Peter was the one who refused to risk following Jesus to the crucifixion. Instead he denied he ever knew Jesus. Peter knew too well the risk of colliding with the Romans. When Jesus was totaled, Peter was left hanging in his seat belt.

I knew allowing my child access to something as powerful as an SUV had its risks. Maybe by denying the collision insurance, I was convincing myself that no harm could come to her. I had my own "Peter moment" when the insurance agent asked me, "Are you sure, Mr. Burkes, that you want to drop this coverage?"

I just didn't want to invest the money necessary to protect

myself against the risk of losing the SUV. I accepted the risk, and I lost.

But something good did come from the wreck; it led me through my own experience of denial—and resurrection. You see, one week after the accident, my daughter walked—or more accurately, limped—across the stage to get her high school diploma. Watching her, it occurred to me there can be no limit to the amount of love I invest in her, and that every bit of risk I take in being her dad is worth it.

And realizing that puts my world right side up.

UNBALANCED PARENTING

As the chaplain for women and children's services at my hospital, I visit a lot of women after they've given birth. Although I've never asked them, I've often wondered whether Cesarean sections or vaginal births are easier. I do know that with many Cesareans, a woman and her doctor can plan and sometimes even schedule the birth, while parents going through "natural" childbirth don't really know when it's going to happen.

Since I'm not a woman, I don't know much about postpartum stuff, except that there's pain with either method. But as a dad, I do know a bit more about *de*parting stuff, which occurs twenty or so years postpartum. I've had two daughters depart the nest, and like women after the birthing experience, I have a few viewpoints to compare.

It's hard to say which departure was easier. One of our daughters left in the spring according to a long-established plan. She was in pursuit of a college degree. Like a planned Cesarean, her departure for college was something we'd always anticipated. There were tears as we watched her go; mostly they were tears for ourselves, knowing we would miss her but feeling happy for her to be taking this next step she had eagerly antici-pated for so long.

In contrast, another daughter made a rather hasty and unscheduled departure in December—all in pursuit of love and independence. Her departure felt premature to us, and we suf-fered all the pain of a birth without anesthesia. This time, our tears were more about our worry for her as she headed down a strange new path we've never traveled. The whole thing puts a big question mark on her future, and question marks are hard to live with.

Back in the hospital, when I watch parents deal with the question mark a premature baby brings to their lives, I hear them say things such as, "I wish someone would give me a crys-tal ball so I'd know the future."

I usually answer that kind of thinking with a question: "What would you do if you knew the future?" In the silence that normally follows, I piggyback another question: "Would you love your baby any less? Would you be any less present in your child's life?"

Of course the answer comes naturally: "No."

Now, I'll admit, there are times when loving a child does *not* come naturally. When he or she is acting out, the first emotion we feel isn't always love. But while the love equation gets a little more complex at this point, it needn't go algebraic.

You remember algebra, right? It's a mathematical system that seeks to balance things on both sides of the equal sign. If we par-ented algebraically, when our children act out in a way that makes them unlovable, we would stop loving them. But Scripture suggests God uses a different, rather unbalanced, system of parenting—and he expects us to follow his lead. Romans 5:8 puts it this way: "God put his love on the line for us by offering his Son in sacrificial death while we were of no use whatever to him" (MSG).

If you go back and read those words again, I think you'll see that God's not into algebra. He has modeled a completely different system, one that guides us through every stage of parenting, from birth through postpartum to "*de*partum." It's a system of unbalanced equations . . . and unconditional love.

WHY MUST I ASK FOR A MIRACLE—AGAIN?

Maybe I'm too old to introduce someone as my "best friend," but that's exactly what I say when I introduce Roger. He has been my best friend for twenty-eight years; we were college roommates and served as best man at each other's wedding.

Roger knows me better than anyone, and one piece of trivia he knows is that I sometimes enjoy teasing folks with the well-placed use of the word *again*. For instance, if someone asks, "When's lunch?" I might reply, "Are you eating *again*?"

If a friend arrives late, confessing a speeding ticket, I might exclaim, "What? *Again*?"

In the mouth of a good comic (or in my case, a talented cynic), *again* is a killer word.

But last year, the word threatened to prove what a killer word it *can* be. It finally lost its humor when it caused me to swerve off the road after hearing my best friend tell me on my cell phone, "Norris, I have cancer again."

Eight years ago doctors diagnosed Roger with acinic cell carcinoma, a rare cancer of the salivary glands. After a surgery that temporarily took away his smile nerves, his surgeon pronounced, "I got it all!"

Well, not quite. The cancer returned, and now additional surgery has again lessened both his smile and his odds for a cure.

Encouraging friends say, "Well, at least you're a chaplain.
You can help him." The problem with that is, while I'm fairly
good at supporting strangers, helping friends scares me to
death. Tears that come from walking with strangers through
painful moments dry quickly, but tears that erupt from walking
with friends through terrifying uncertainty flow like an unceas-
ing spring.

The latest treatment has brought promising results. But I
worry the cancer might return again. Is it possible, I wonder, that
Roger's luck may run out? Is luck—good or bad—limited by
some quota? I wish I could promise Roger that Scripture limits
tragedy in his life like a grocery sale: two for five dollars, but the
limit is four. If I had my way, the quota would be more like a challenging adventure: cancer, completely curable—lifetime limit one
per customer.

Through my years of working in a hospital, I've watched
several families hear the word *again* as they've been pushed far
beyond what would seem like a lifetime limit of tragedies:

A police officer mourns the loss of a brother and then is told
she must plan a funeral—again—for her only child.

A heart patient struggles for life—again—but this time loses
to a totally unrelated cancer.

The mother of a young son receives the Mother's Day news
that her child has cancer—again.

It's dizzying, and it brings another word to the forefront:
why?

A friend tells me the only answer to *Why?* is . . . *Because.* I
find that answer wholly unsatisfying but, unable to discover a

better one, I've stopped trying to figure it out. Instead, I'm changing my focus, and that change feels like a miracle in itself. And so, as life begins to be less and less about *Again?* and *Why?* it's becoming more and more about *What?—What, Lord? What are you telling me in this?*

It's less about the destination and more about the journey itself. And with that refocus has come a shifting away from the worrisome future and more into the miracles of the moment— and a greater awareness of the God who accompanies me through every moment, no matter what it holds.

While I am praying for Roger to be cancer free and for his smile to return—again—I know there is no guarantee about the outcome. I can only promise to be there with him in the struggle. It's much the same promise God made to us as he encouraged us to seek the kingdom of God within ourselves and to know, as Scripture promises, that he will be with us "even unto the end of the world" (Matthew 28:20 KJV).

And I'm still walking with Roger, much like I walk with other patients—only in his case I use a bit more Kleenex. And each day Roger returns to the hospital for another treatment, his cell phone rings, and he knows it's me—again.

"Hey, Roger? How about lunch?" I ask.

To which he replies, "Again?"

HEARTS SOFTEN IN A SMALL BED

In my days as a military chaplain, I moved a lot, and I took each move as an opportunity to shed some of my worldly stuff.

OK, I confess. Sometimes these shedding times were actually just a ruse to update my material world. For example, before one recent move, I had big plans to ditch our queen-size bed and buy a new king-size waterbed with dual heaters. But my wife nixed that idea, saying we didn't need a king-size anything. I tried to explain it using the Chaplain Norris paraphrase of the *Field of Dreams* principle. Instead of, "If you build it, they will come," I like to say, "If we buy it, I will grow."

My wife will tell you my real problem is not the size of the bed but my constant movement that propels me to every corner of the mattress by night's end. She should really buy me one of those adjustable beds that promise the flexibility of a hospital bed; surely all those possibilities for sleeping positions would eliminate my all-night squirming.

But the truth is, hospital beds aren't made to be comfortable. In fact, in this time of managed care, if your discharge planner could prove a bed of nails would allow a quick discharge, you would have one as soon as you're admitted.

And don't even think about finding comfort in an emergency room. Think gurney—in some places, eight hours of gurney. Those overworked ER staff want you to think twice before coming to them with a stomachache. An honest charge nurse will just come out and tell you, "It's the flu, honey. Get over it, or enjoy your gurney because you're going to be there awhile!"

No, my advice is, when you're shopping for beds, don't buy anything comparable to a hospital bed. I see a lot of people in hospital beds, and they rarely seem comfortable—especially when two are sharing the bed, as was one such couple I encountered. I must admit that while they didn't seem comfortable, it was rare to encounter a couple who radiated such beauty. It happened when a nurse directed me to the room of an elderly man who had died.

The new widow was there with her family, and the room was filled with pictures and mementos that intentionally communicated to the staff this man was not to be identified by a mere room number or a diagnosis. His family wanted us to know he had a name and a life, as well as a family who loved him. I entered the room to find the body of a man slight enough to allow his wife room to perch on the corner of the mattress. She leaned into his stiff, sagging shoulder and held his hand while caressing his arm. His eyes were closed, and his mouth open.

As I sat and talked with the family, the wife told me that for nearly six decades she and this man had shared a bed—always a double bed, not a queen or a king. Now she was wondering how cold and lonely the nights would get without him.

"I just can't understand it," she said. "So many of our friends buy these big beds. They say they need the room. But the beds are so big, you lose each other!"

She made her friends' beds sound like the Grand Canyon, not a simple king-size waterbed with dual heaters, I noted rather defensively.

She told me there was always enough room in their bed, because from the moment they first slid in all those years ago, their emotional compass had been set on lifelong commitment. In the center of their bed each night, they found each other's hand, and so entwined, peaceful sleep came easily.

Now, in front of us that afternoon, a permanent peace had also come easily—at least for one of them. The new widow would have some grief work to do, but we knew that, at her advanced age, she was likely to join him soon in a place where their souls would become permanently entwined.

In that room it occurred to me that while I had seen the pageantry of many formal weddings, it was rare to see the beauty I was witnessing here: the final fulfillment of vows taken by a couple who had meant what they said when they promised "for better or for worse, 'til death do us part."

Through the years, I have heard a lot of reasons for breaking those vows. Perhaps Jesus identified the real reason when he explained that Moses had only approved the breaking of marital vows because of the hardness of the people's hearts (see Matthew 19:8). Surely during their fifty-eight years this man and wife had moments when anger, frustration, or worries had hardened their hearts, at least temporarily. But somehow, they had discovered that hard hearts are softened in smaller beds.

In my family's most recent move, we somehow managed to bring most of our stuff without shedding much of anything. Everything from Tinkertoys to washing machines was loaded into the moving van. And somewhere in there, wedged between a dresser and the washing machine, was an old queen bed, our nightly meeting place for years to come.

SEARCH AND RESCUE IN WAL-MART

As I arrived home late from work, my wife met me at the door and spun me back around.

"The kids need school supplies," she said. "I need you to take them to Wal-Mart."

"I don't know what they want," I answered, pitching my voice into a husbandly whine.

"They have a list," she retorted. "And they're ready to go."

It wasn't the way I had planned to spend the evening. But then I remembered Wal-Mart's electronics department: amps, volts, watts, and gigabytes, a paradise of geek testosterone.

"Fine," I said with a twinkle of mischievous revenge in my eye. "I have my own list."

Arriving at Wal-Mart, the two school-supply shoppers and I headed for our separate corners of the store. Quickly finding the store's audiovisual heaven, a place wallpapered with HDTVs, I fell into a trance. But in a few moments a TV news story jerked me back to reality. Remains were being recovered of two missing thirteen-year-old Oregon girls.

My anxiety meter suddenly shot up ten points: time to find my thirteen-year-old son and his fifteen-year-old sister. Rushing to the scene of their expected spending spree, I found empty shelves and floors carpeted with erasers, rulers, and pens. I was sure they had been there, but they weren't there anymore.

Finding my daughter was easy because I knew where to look. Heeding an invisible radar, sort of like a horse that loses its rider and returns to the ranch, when a teenage daughter loses her brother and father in a discount store, she heads for cosmetics.

Finding my son was harder. First, I doubled back to the electronics department, hoping to confirm the adage, "Like father, like son." Nope. He wasn't there. But there *was* another news story blasting from the wall of HDTVs announcing the guilty verdict imposed on the killer of some teenagers in Yosemite National Park.

My breathing grew shallow, and my pace quickened. I was praying that the fear I was feeling was going to be the worst part of my day and that reality would soon bring relief.

Where is he?

Perhaps the outdoor department . . . no, not there.

Walking again toward the front of the store, I asked the electronics cashier to page my son again. "This time use his last name," I requested, hoping public humiliation would work.

Five minutes later, no response. Another news story erupted

from the dozens of screens plastering the electronics department. Closed caption told me what I could not hear over the pounding panic in my ears: a child killer was being sentenced somewhere in Southern California.

My fear came closer to the surface now. I was starting to wonder at what point one calls the police. By now my daughter and I had combed every inch of the store, and I had asked each cashier I passed, "Could you page him again, please?"

Five times I made this request.

Then, just as I thought my anxiety had reached maximum level, my hospital pager went off. The NICU was requesting prayer for a baby before they removed the breathing machines. "I'll be there within the hour," I replied, trying to conceal the mounting fear that was blocking any concern I might have for anyone else's child.

Twenty minutes had passed since the first page. I anchored myself at the customer service counter and asked yet another associate, "Please page him once more—and speak louder."

Then, uneventfully, my son strolled up to me as though he had just paused to tie his shoe. He had been in the bathroom.

Losing a kid in Wal-Mart cannot compare to the unspeakable tragedies many parents have known. Yet their tragic stories have put fear on a hair trigger for the rest of us dads and moms. A misplaced kid in the grocery store used to mean little more than an inconvenient delay in shopping. Now it sends fear soaring to the surface.

Jesus told a parable, beginning in Luke 15, about a man whose son broke free of parental ties to go on his own shopping spree. When the son asked for it, the father gave him his rightful inheritance and allowed him to depart for another country. Once there, the son spent his inheritance on riotous living, Jesus said. The parable says that while the son was still far off, his father found him. To me, that means the father was searching for him.

Always searching.

Before his son grew penniless and repentant from eating hog slop, the father left home to look for his son. That was the remarkable thing. His father wasn't waiting on the front porch (or at the customer service counter); he was actively involved in the search for his lost son.

When you consider the unspeakable terror of 9/11, compounded by recent high-profile crimes that have been perpetrated on children, parents seem justified in sometimes feeling overwhelmed by fear. But while we are well advised to seek God in all circumstances, especially in times of high anxiety, we need to heed the lesson this parable makes clear: God first sought us, and is still seeking for us. He seeks us so he might demonstrate that, in the midst of our fear, in the ache of our loss, we have not lost—and cannot lose everything. He is there, his love is constant, and he will help us see there is still much love remaining in the world. Let us never focus so fiercely on what we have lost that we are unable to remember the love of what we have remaining.

When I returned home, my son figured he would be grounded for the length of his natural life, but instead he got a hug he didn't quite understand. As for my daughter, she had a request.

"Mom," she begged, "can *you* take us shopping next time? Dad gets too uptight."

FAITH WAVERS IN THE DENTIST'S CHAIR

When I read about alleged mistreatment of Taliban leaders detained at Guantanamo, I was sure those allegations were groundless—until I heard the detainees would be receiving dental care. I know Amnesty International would agree: dental treatment is torture.

There is no place I hate to be more than the dentist's office, but there I sat in his waiting room once again.

I have a triad strategy for facing pain: denial, deflection, or distraction. During that visit, I chose distraction. I pulled out my Palm Pilot, docked it to the portable keyboard, placed it on a borrowed clipboard, and began typing out this solicitation for your sympathy. I knew divine power had brought me into that waiting room, but I would leave it a weak-kneed shell of a saint. I sit in the waiting room both before *and after* a dental appointment. I wait before because even a man of God waits for a doctor or dentist, and I wait afterward to recollect my halo as my nausea wears off.

I come to this proving ground of faith for dental work—and also to put my spirituality through its paces. If my faith is going to break down, it will be here. I know it, and the dental staff knows it too. They enjoy watching the chaplain slink into the office, sink into the chair, and have his faith pushed to the brink. I feel them mocking me. I imagine them asking, "Where is your God now, Chaplain? Where is the amazing scriptural peace you claim as being 'beyond understanding'?"

I dunno, I might answer, maybe my peace choked on that cardboard X-ray film holder you stuffed into my throat.

Or maybe my faith is jerked out of me by that fishhook the hygienist uses to clean my teeth. If he offered me a choice of letting him scrape my molars with that hook or allowing him to shove a garden rake into my mouth, I think I would choose the rake. At least it would be over sooner.

But he offers me no such choice, and the procedure is never over quickly. The reason is the industrial-size bags of fried starch I buy at McDonald's; those delicious french fries take their toll on my dental health by forming a bulletproof shield of plaque. As a result, it sometimes takes two sessions to clean my teeth.

My only consolation is that I use these times to release my hostilities; the dental chair is the one place where I can swear freely. It's like the old adage that asks whether a tree falling in the woods makes a sound if nobody can hear it. If a chaplain starts swearing, but no one can understand him, it doesn't count, right?

Maybe, like me, you encounter situations where publicly demonstrating your faith is a challenging spiritual struggle. As a chaplain, I would tell you this desire to maintain a godly facade comes from our own vanities and not from God; but as a human being I have to acknowledge that it's easier said than done. Most of us just can't help trying to be the person other people think we are.

Fortunately, there are usually people around us who know how to deflate our righteous pretentiousness, clip our angel wings, and reduce us to being human just like everyone else. For me that person is the dentist—even if I'm not the one in the chair.

For example, my daughter recently had oral surgery to repair a birth defect, a procedure requiring her jaw to be broken in six places. The week after the surgery, I began to obsess about her progress during recovery, imagining the worst of possibilities. So I called the oral surgeon to grill him about what was happening. I'm sure the surgeon heard the fear in my voice, and

I suspect he also heard a lack of faith in a person who is supposed to be a faith-focused professional. He couldn't see in me the God I so strongly desire to reflect. But he did see through my weak humanity. He heard in my phone call the voice of a scared dad, and he responded with kind reassurance.

It's funny how hard we work to project the image of what we imagine ourselves to be—and how miserably we fail at it. It's funny, too, to realize we count ourselves too smart to be fooled by others' façades, but we are certain they are too dumb to see through ours.

Yes, the dentist can see through my perfect-man-of-God demeanor to detect the cavities in my façade. But he's not the only one. My wife, children, friends, and colleagues see through it too. They can hear the tree that falls in the forest, because sometimes it falls on them. They can hear the rage that sometimes erupts in me and the inconsistencies that sometimes mar my message, and they can sense my wavering faith that sometimes impairs the vision I wish they had of me.

Yet they keep loving and accepting me in a way that reflects the love and acceptance of God—who, even more so, sees our most secret flaw and continues to love and accept us. While I know the dentist is not the only one who can see through my façade, I keep hoping he will be the last. He seems to know that the title of the Twila Paris song is true: this "warrior is a child." Maybe that is why the dentist talks to me the way he does.

"Now, this might hurt just an eeency-weency bit," he warns.

"Are you a pediatric dentist too?" I ask.

"Why, yes, I am. What makes you ask?"

"Maybe your Mr. Rogers voice," I suggest. "Ouch! %$#%$#%#!"

"Pardon me, Chaplain? What did you say?"

"Nvr mnd."

Before every trip to the dentist, I mull over the fact that the Bible says God doesn't like unclean lips, but it says nothing about unclean teeth. If it was so important, you'd think God would have mentioned it somewhere . . .

ARE YOU MY DAUGHTER?

When I saw you yesterday on the freeway on-ramp, I thought you looked a lot like my teenage daughter. You saw me, didn't you? I squinted to read the handwritten sign you held so tightly, wondering what you wanted. Your sign seemed much like the signs kids your age hold to advertise a car wash.

But there was no car wash. I could see you were alone: no friends, no support. You only had your sign. My car crept closer in the traffic as the onslaught of commuters awaited the go light that would launch us toward our homes and our dinner.

Finally I was close enough to read the sign. The letters were thin; the sign was wrinkled. I couldn't read your sign in time to stop. Couldn't you have made bigger letters? Please, get a bigger sign next time! When I could finally read your sign, I saw that it said Bay Area.

Driving you to San Francisco Bay would have added another four hours to my commute. How could I possibly have helped you? And the bay area is huge. Where in the bay area did you want to go? You didn't act like it mattered. Would anywhere do? Has your life come to mean so little in your short time on earth that you'd settle for going anywhere?

What if I had taken you where you wanted to go, but once

you were there you ended up worse than you are now? Would I be a conspirator in your pain? Would I want some well-meaning guy taking my daughter away from her family because she had a sign and she reminded him of his daughter?

But it wasn't even your sign that had most of my attention. It was your stare.

You stared first into my car to measure the room I had for you. But you also seemed to notice that I had little room for you in my heart; I wasn't slowing down. In fact, I was speeding ahead. I wouldn't be the one who would help you today.

But you didn't just look into my car. Our eyes locked. You looked into me and you knew, didn't you? You knew I had a daughter your age, and you could see the fear I had for you.

Did you see the hesitancy in my eyes? Did you notice the uncertainty with which my brake lights flashed as I scanned the ramp for a way to stop? There are no U-turns on a freeway ramp, or I swear, I'd have come back for you. But with traffic at a stand-still, you would surely have found your ride before I had a chance to return. Still, I wish I had gone back and checked on you. I thought about you all the way home; I wish I knew you made it safely to your destination.

But it wasn't just you that I thought of on my drive home. I also thought of a conversation I'd had with a doctor that day.

"Chaplain, as you watch all the pain around us," the doctor asked, "does it ever make you want to become an atheist? I mean, what purpose does all this pain serve?"

"Hm-mmm," I replied, stalling.

Later, thinking of you, I too wondered, *What purpose does your pain serve, my hitchhiking daughter?*

I can't answer the question; I can't be responsible for how your pain will shape you, affect you. But I *am* responsible for how your pain will affect *me*.

And maybe, somewhere out there, it's affecting a reader right now too.

FALLING TO THE OBVIOUS CONCLUSION

Being a syndicated newspaper columnist, as well as a full-time chaplain, gives me a new perspective on occurrences in my life that might otherwise be seen as downers. For example, if I weren't a columnist, I might have been completely distraught when I backed my SUV into a wall. But the silver lining was that at least I had something new to write about that week. Describing that experience allowed me to share with my readers a sense of the suffering I had to endure each week to come up with new material for my column.

The week after the fender bender, my suffering on behalf of my readers continued as I undertook a day of mountain biking. Now, let me begin by saying that I've owned a mountain bike for twenty years, but recently I bought a new one. I don't know why exactly, but somehow my new purchase made me feel obligated to actually try mountain biking. (Up until then my mountain biking had been limited to the incline of my driveway.) So when my hospital-social-worker friend Jennifer invited my college-age daughter, Sara, and me to do some real riding, I jumped at the opportunity to test my fantasy: I owned a mountain bike; therefore, I *was* a mountain biker. No problem.

But to be a real mountain biker, you need mountain-biker shoes, the kind that lock onto the pedals. Seeing them, my wife cautioned me to be careful. "Those things don't seem like such a good idea, Norris," she warned. "It's like putting a seat belt on a motorcycle. What happens if you have to stop? You'll fall dead on your face."

"Ah, honey, I'll be all right," I assured her. After all, Becky doesn't really know much about mountain biking. "They're no problem," I said, placating her worries. "I've got it all figured out."

So off we went, and after a half mile of chasing the twenty-six-year-old, athletic Jennifer up the mountain trail, my forty-something heart ran out of steam. In a Kodak moment right out of the movie *Clockstoppers*, I froze precariously—right on a teetering rock. The thought suddenly occurred to me, *This would be the moment my prophetess wife predicted.*

With my feet locked in my pedals, I glanced in terror at the rocks below, realizing they would be my resting place for a while (and praying they wouldn't be my *final* resting place). Then I closed my eyes and braced for impact.

When my body had landed and my head had cleared, I was wondering two things. First, *Did Jennifer hear what I said as I fell?* If she were on a covert mission from the Baptist hierarchy to find out if my cussing was out of control, this would have been an ingenious test.

The second thing I wondered was, *Do social workers get first-aid training?*

Apparently not. As she extended her hand without so much as a cold compress, it became obvious that the only thing she knew was how to drag me out of the way of the other bikers who were screaming down the trail. Which, on second thought, wasn't such a bad idea.

I'm not sure if it was after that first fall onto the rocks or my second fall into poison oak or my third fall into some shrubbery, but at some point I started wondering what God wanted me to learn from the mountain-biking experience: *What is your will, Lord? Do you want me to break* all *my bones? What wisdom are you trying to impart that I might share with others?*

So far, the only clues I had were a bruised rib, an exposed ego, and a cell phone that took my falls almost as badly as I did.

Amazingly, some people have called me dense, but sometime after I saw the fearless Jennifer fly over her handlebars, cracking her helmet three times, I actually began to hear God's message to me. Amazingly, he sounded a lot like my wife: *You don't know how to mountain bike, and you are too old to learn!* (I'll be forty-something-plus-one in a few months. Send birthday checks to defray medical expenses in care of the publisher.)

Although I survived learning this lesson, the mystery of my misery was compounded when I caught a cold a few days later, and every time I sneezed, my bruised rib sharply reminded me of God's will: *learn how before you actually go.* Even my chiropractor is on his side. He told me if I ever repeat that stupid stunt, my insurance wouldn't cover preexisting idiocy.

There are those who think that God's will is discerned exclusively through Bible reading, prayer, and church attendance. While I fully commend those things to you, I also acknowledge other aids and helpers in discerning God's will for our individual lives.

For me, one of them was the late Christian comedian Grady Nutt, who complained that people sometimes describe surrendering to God's will as something like surrendering to an enemy soldier. Nutt reasoned that surrendering to God's will ought to be something far more natural and simple. For instance, he said he was certain God wouldn't want him to be a mother, and that on most days, he was equally certain God didn't want him to be a ballerina.

Nutt's helmet wasn't cracked; he was dead on. It's a full-time job, Nutt reasoned, just doing the acts of love required to be one of Christ's followers without spending years selfishly sleuthing out his specific will for our unique situations. Doing the things we know to be right is what Jesus described as seeking the kingdom of God. If we seek first his kingdom, Jesus said, all the important things we need will be given to us (see Matthew 6:28–33).

Incidentally, I did the SUV thing again soon after the mountain-biking misadventure. This time I backed into the car of a fellow churchgoer at a huge church where we had been considering membership. "No damage this time," I sheepishly reported to my wife, "but I think God must be telling us to look for another church."

Again the prophetess spoke: "I think God is trying to tell you to check *all* your mirrors before you back up."

Sometimes God's will can be all too obvious.

A GOOD MARRIAGE REQUIRES SWEAT

I've done a lot of premarital counseling, and while it's a serious endeavor, it's also fraught with comic fodder because of the funny notions couples often have. Once, a few days after helping a couple make wedding arrangements, I had a chance encounter with the groom-to-be. We exchanged a passing greeting, then he did an about-face and tossed a "by-the-way" bomb.

"Did I mention that my fiancée doesn't want to promise 'till death do us part'?" he asked. "Would that be a deal breaker?"

Déjà vu.

Two years earlier, a bride-to-be had asked to change the vows to "till love do us part." Five months later, the groom left on a navy cruise and her love "parted" so she could switch to a land lover.

I gave both couples the same answer: "Uh, you know what? I'm afraid I have to stick with the unabridged format."

Unfortunately, marriage counseling is far less comedic and much more frustrating than premarriage counseling. To be honest, the most frustrating thing is that I've been blessed with a marriage I can't clone in others.

Oftentimes when I've come home after counseling with a couple, my wife greets me with a hug and she instantly feels my frustration in my return embrace. Having just witnessed the carnage marriage can sometimes be, I hold her tight. For me, there is no greater priority on earth than my marriage. Why would anyone take risks with his or her marriage by making it analogous to hell?

But those risks are taken every day, and I often see the results of them in the counseling sessions. A hospital worker once burst in my office and proclaimed, "Chaplain! Chaplain! She said yes! She said yes!"

The man had been dating another hospital employee for two years and had finally popped the question. I knew them both well and figured their biggest challenge would be to quit smoking. (Despite what health-care workers witness, some smoke like chimneys.)

He heralded the news from floor to floor until he arrived in the basement—literally and figuratively. Upon arriving in the unit where his *old* girlfriend was the shift manager, she gave him a congratulatory hug. Then she invited him into a closet, where she "congratulated" him a bit more thoroughly. In a hot Texas minute, a two-year relationship went up in smoke. And the hospital administration congratulated the closet lovers with some unpaid vacation.

Before my father-in-law performed our wedding ceremony, he asked Becky and me a series of questions—the same questions he has asked hundreds of couples. One of them was about fidelity. He asked each of us, "How many times could the other be unfaithful before you would seek divorce?" He was making the point that marriage isn't solely about sex, and sex should not break it apart.

At first it seemed that Becky did not understand the point of the question, but the fact was, she was making another point. With the back of her hand facing me, she held up five fingers. At first I thought, *This could be interesting. She's allowing for five indiscretions apiece? Would churches hire a minister with such an open marriage?*

Slowly she rolled down her fingers until her hand formed a fist. Then she shook the fist in my direction and said, "This many times, buddy. This many times!"

Becky had given me a glimpse of how much risk she would tolerate.

When you see people like the hospital workers risking something so precious, it shakes you. You try to define and categorize what you have, believe that if you can define it, you can control and guard it so that nothing can destroy it.

Still, I'm not entirely sure what kind of marriage my wife and I have. I do know it is the kind of love that keeps on going whether I burn the toast or burn my temper with my children. It is the kind of love that tells me I am forgiven before I can ask. It is the kind of love the wedding vow describes that "halves a sorrow and doubles a joy."

Like many couples, we sometimes go to bed dead tired—sometimes too tired for the fun I seek and too tired for the prayer she requests. But we are rarely too tired to talk about our day and absolutely never too tired for our traditional three good-night kisses and an "I love you."

Maybe I know a thing about marriages that the hospital workers know about smokers. Watching them die doesn't make you any less disposed to becoming one of them. If you want to quit smoking, it takes work, and even then you may not succeed. Watching marriages die has made our marriage no more likely to succeed. We know marriage takes work.

Maybe there is something Freudian about the way my fast fingers always mistype *sweetheart* into *sweatheart*. A good marriage takes a lot of work and a great deal of spiritual sweat.

I love you, sweatheart!

CHURCH HOPPING

When I left my ministry and faith community in the Air National Guard to return to civilian hospital ministry, I faced the challenge of finding a new place of worship. As an active-duty military chaplain I had led worship services in the chapel at an air force base. Now that I was back out in the civilian world, I needed a civilian church. As I began my search, I quickly found that it wasn't too different from what Disney advertisers call (I'm raising my fingers in that annoying quote sign) "park hopping." I called my efforts (here go the fingers again) "church hopping."

Church hoppers are shoppers who are looking for that perfect church. They want a youth group for Johnny, a children's program for Sissy, and a nursery with closed-circuit television monitors and daddy pagers. Add to the shopping list a preacher who isn't too boring and a music program that rocks, plus pews with first-class legroom. Throw in Big Gulp communion cups, and you have the perfect church.

My problem is that when I go church hopping, I'm the insider who knows too much. I become like the meat packer who won't eat bologna or the chef who becomes a food critic. Knowing too much can be brutal. My critical eye spots the pastor reading a sermon—especially one he didn't write. I don't need a revelation to know when the music minister and the pastor are not in harmony, and when I see ushers smoking at the back of the sanctuary I don't have to be clairvoyant to know the church is having a problem.

My wife will tell you that this critical attitude of mine will prevent me from ever being totally happy in my new church. I'm like a sidelined quarterback, and from that ecclesiastical sideline I wonder things like, *Where did this guy get his degree?* Or, *Does she really think she can pull off a forty-five-minute sermon or is she going to quit when the guy in front of me falls asleep and cracks his skull on the pew?*

I'm always thinking I could write a better sermon or even take the pastor's own manuscript and preach it much better myself. I daydream about the good old days when I was preaching weekly sermons. They were never boring because I wrote them fresh (and sometimes a little frantic), every Saturday night.

When I get too critical, my wife reminds me that in those good old days, I sometimes had to write as many as three sermons a week. She would frequently find me sleeping on my desk and ask, "How do you expect the congregation to stay awake if you fall asleep writing your own sermon?" Now, I have to admit, that was always a stumper.

Still, I'm human, and I will probably church shop 'til I drop. Like many, I will look for a place where my teenager might actually sing, a church I will want to invite my neighbor to. I'll keep looking for a church where a congregation member won't cut me off as I'm pulling into one of the guest parking spaces.

Some folks don't see the point in church at all; they tell me I can have a spiritual life without a spiritual community. But I tell them I have about as much chance of maintaining spiritual glow outside a faith community as a spark has of maintaining its glow sitting alone on the fireplace hearth.

I once visited a patient who had just undergone surgery to remove a tumor from his brain. The procedure was extensive, and his survival was questionable. I introduced myself and asked if he would like me to pray for him. He nodded, and then he whispered something. I strained to listen, barely able to make out his words: "Teach *me* to pray," he said.

At that moment, I was struck by the fact that his simple request combined both the most rewarding element of my job with the most tragic. While it was humbling to be asked to teach this man such an intimate thing as prayer, it was also sad that he had to make his request of a stranger. The most tragic part of being a hospital chaplain is not the human suffering I see on a daily basis; it's watching people struggle through suffering without a connection to a faith community. That is why I am determined not to be without one.

Other folks try to discourage my church-hopping search by complaining that there are too many hypocrites in the church. I tell them the church is a place where people gather on a weekly basis to acknowledge their imperfections. In fact, they celebrate the fact that they are far less than perfect.

I like to explain it this way: searching for the *perfect* church filled with *perfect* people worshiping *perfectly* is not the point of finding a faith community. The point is having a community that will welcome us, love us in our imperfection, pick us up when we stumble, laugh with us through our joys, and cry with us through our pain. As I see it, the miracle is the imperfect community of imperfect people loving each other in spite of their unlovable parts.

So I want to find a group of people who take comfort in the fact that we are all sinners, and who assemble together because none are perfect. Indeed, I hope to find a church that will be something like an Alcoholics Anonymous meeting, where I can introduce myself by saying, "Hi, I'm Norris. I'm fairly messed up, and I'm going to need a place to worship."

When my heart hears that chorus of "Hi, Norris!" in response, then I'll know I'm home.

SEEING BOTH SIDES OF BEAUTY

It was a $2.4 million fumble from Ford Motor Company: a 2005 Super Bowl ad you didn't see because it was canceled after complaints by victims of clergy sexual abuse. In the commercial, the minister finds truck keys in the collection plate and the new truck, a Lincoln Mark LT, in the parking lot. Thinking he's just become the beneficiary of a generous act of charity, the minister starts caressing the truck, admiring its sleek lines and luxurious interior. Just then a congregant and his daughter arrive to explain how the young girl accidentally dropped the keys in the collection plate. In the closing scene, the minister is seen posting the next week's sermon title: "Lust."

In all the years I pastored, I don't think I ever preached a sermon on lust. I suppose I knew a good sermon starts best with your own confessions—and I wasn't going there. But as a Christian writer, I have a confession to make: lust is a familiar feeling, as familiar as last week.

It was my weekend for National Guard duty, so I ducked into a downtown barbershop, where I met a barber who was definitely not my father's barber. This barber was pleasant, energetic, and . . . gorgeous.

When I requested a military haircut, she asked if I was a pilot. I'll admit, there was a lustful part of me that wanted to be. Pretty pathetic, huh? No, I'm not a candidate for sainthood; however, my wife has proofread this manuscript and approves this message.

Lust is the easy substitute for honest relationships. It's really about categorizing people and wanting them to fit into the image you've created for them. It's about refusing them exit from the fantasy in which you've imprisoned them. The problem is, that prison quickly becomes *your* prison.

And in case any of this is sounding like wise advice, let me tell you, wisdom has a way of escaping a man sitting in a barber chair enjoying young hands combing through thin and graying hair. Nevertheless, I somehow managed a thought about the real person in the mirror behind me and squeaked out a question. Noticing her wedding ring, and twirling my own, I asked, "Do you have kids?"

"Yes, two," she said. "They're eight and five." She was thirty-two years old and had been married nine years. She migrated from Vietnam ten years ago, learned the language, and started a hairstyling business.

Hearing her story, my thoughts wandered away from her beauty to the challenges she had overcome. I couldn't help but imagine the communist bureaucracy she had battled and how it must have ostracized her. Gradually, the beauty that had attracted my gaze was more toward the center of this person and the heart of her courage.

She had come to this country alone and later brought her parents. Now she waits for a sister to navigate the post-9/11 red tape, and she has ideas of expediting the process by finding the sister a husband. If the sisters look alike, I thought, that shouldn't be a problem.

I was still struggling to rein in my thoughts, but I let her continue her story. She had waited years to be approved for immigration until finally someone believed in her and sponsored her to come to America. Now she struggles to make a living, raise a family, and find sponsors for her remaining family members. She misses them enormously.

As the young woman's story called me out of the original depiction I had created for her, I recalled the words of the apostle Paul in 1 Thessalonians 4:4, when he urged his readers to "appreciate and give dignity" to the human body, adding, in verse 7, "God hasn't invited us into a disorderly, unkempt life but into something holy and beautiful—as beautiful on the inside as the outside" (MSG).

She finished cutting my hair. I doubled the usual tip. I'm not sure why I did that—a guilt offering maybe? I'm hoping it was more about finally seeing the real person. But truthfully, as I'm still human, it will probably always be a bit of both.

JUST WHEN WE NEED IT, A LAUGH

The tragedies I see in the hospital sometimes seem like a soap-opera script or the lyrics to a country song. A natural result of having witnessed these tragedies is the quick anxiety I develop when a family member is late coming home.

It happened again last week. An hour late, my wife returned home portraying herself as the Good Samaritan who had helped a stranded motorist. I've told her the parable of the Good Samaritan has gotten more do-gooders killed than any other Bible story.

The story I share here is the tale she told me upon her late arrival, and as wild as it is, she's sticking to it.

Becky said she noticed a college-age girl stranded in her packed VW convertible alongside a four-lane boulevard near our house. (And did I mention that the temperature that day maxed out at about 104?) With our own daughter set to make an eight-hundred-mile college migration soon, Becky's impending empty-nest syndrome combined with Good Samaritan guilt motivated her to stop. The VW's top was down, and the bug was obviously packed with college-dorm-room stuff. On the folded-down top, strapped under bungee-cord netting, was a bicycle.

"Are you having trouble?" my wife inquired.

Becky might have anticipated a wide variety of answers, but the one she got wasn't among them: "Yes, I am," the girl said. "I can't get the pig back in his kennel."

That's when my wife noticed movement under the netting. Trapped under the bungee-cord netting, inside the bicycle-frame maze, was one scared pig.

"Oh. A pig," Becky answered. Not knowing much about pigs and unsure how to help, she wondered why the pig had to be moved.

"Can't it just stay up there?" she asked.

"Well, maybe," the girl speculated. "But do you think it can travel four hundred miles on the freeway like that?"

My wife admitted the pig probably wouldn't like that.

"Let's try to push it back into the crate," she suggested.

As the duo pushed, poked, prodded, and pulled to navigate the animal through the bike frame and out from under the bungee net, the pig let out horrendous squeals. (One thing Becky now knows about pigs is that they can be extremely loud. I don't know much about pigs either, but that was the one fact I'd heard years earlier. When I attended Baylor, we were told that pigs were so loud our archrivals, the Texas A&M Aggies, used them for car alarms.)

But back to our story: Worried that the pig was beginning to foam at the mouth, my wife was losing her motivation to touch the mammal. Loud, stinky, and now menacingly threatening her with (no doubt) an infectious disease, the pig seemed to be pushing this roadside scenario off the *Candid Camera* set and into a *Twilight Zone* situation.

And then things got worse. Suddenly the terrified pig leapt from his perch, and bolted across four lanes of busy Labor Day traffic.

Now, you have to understand, this happened in California. I've seen traffic back up for geese, dogs, and skunks, but stopping for a pig would strain the patience of even the best tree-hugging Californians I know. Ignoring the danger and still determined to make good her offer of help, Becky sprung into action. She threw her arms up quicker than a charismatic in a tent revival meeting and brought four lanes of traffic to a screeching halt while the young lady darted after her pig. Cars were careening, and bacon was squealing as the young girl cornered her pig in some roadside bushes.

As my wife crossed the street to join them, she overheard the girl ask herself, "How do I get myself into these things?"

"I was just thinking the same thing," Becky mumbled.

The pig was trapped in the bushes, but he wasn't caught, and the women were losing confidence in their ability to capture him. They began to examine their options.

"I guess I should call the owner," the girl concluded, "but she doesn't have a car."

"This pig isn't yours?" my wife responded incredulously.

"No, it belongs to a friend, and I promised to bring it to UC San Diego for her brother," she answered. Then she said again, "How *do* I get myself into these messes?"

This Good Samaritan story had gone terribly wrong, but Becky saw a way to extract herself.

"Call your friend," she commanded, "and I'll go pick her up."

Suspicious at my wife's generosity, the girl asked, "You'd do that?"

In a heartbeat, my wife thought as she forced out an audibly courteous, "Certainly."

Moments later, my wife returned with the friend and quickly accepted the two girls' dismissive assurances that now they would be fine.

Throughout this book I've tried to include spiritual lessons in my stories, but the only pig-related Bible story I know is about a demon-possessed herd running off a cliff as their owners tried to retrieve them. And, as demon-possessed as this pig may have seemed, it would be forcing a point to parallel that story.

However, the experience did leave Becky and me with an important lesson. This roadside adventure occurred on Labor Day weekend 2002, just a few days before the first anniversary of the 9/11 attacks. As we struggled, along with the rest of America, to absorb the devastating impact of the loss our nation had suffered, the hurt that had been inflicted, we had a fresh, little bright spot to remember during those darkest days immediately following the attack. It reminded us that, even in the difficult moments, we need to hold on to our God-given ability to laugh. As we went through the healing process, we trusted our Creator to heal our hearts and continue to give us moments in life that reflect the divine smile placed in us all.

ALMOST HELPING

My father had a great deal of love for children; I think that's where I got a lot of my own playfulness. Growing up as a pastor's kid, most church events were mandatory for me, and Vacation Bible School (VBS in church lingo) was one of them. After all, if the pastor's kid failed to show up, all the other kids would use my absence as their own excuse to pitch a wailing fit about having to go.

For a long time, I thought the best thing about Vacation Bible School was the "summer missionaries," usually very pretty, soft-spoken college girls who had been sent by our southern-based denomination to save the West. The missionaries usually stayed with our family, and if I was lucky, they would teach my fifth-grade boys' class. Each year I became so hooked on the charm of their southern accents, I once again gave God my solemn vow to become a minister. What a great debt I owe to those pretty girls.

VBS was filled with girls who wanted to give their hearts to Jesus and boys who wanted to give their hearts to the summer missionaries. It had the potential to bring out the entire community, and attendees were encouraged to invite friends from their school and the neighborhood. We called those kids "prospects," and for each prospect I recruited, I'd get a candy bar.

One day, a neighborhood prospect named Stevie was playing at my house when my dad suggested he come to Vacation Bible School. With visions of candy bars dancing in my head, I enthusiastically endorsed the idea—in fact, claimed it as my own.

Stevie was almost my friend but not really. We lacked the solid connection that would move us beyond acquaintance status. Stevie lived on Twenty-first Street and was almost my neighbor. His backyard was only a few parcels short of bordering mine. My family was almost as big as his. His had six, and mine had five. He was almost my age. I was ten, and he was nine. I could swim, and Stevie could almost swim.

My parents loved me, and his parents almost loved him.

There were so many *almosts* with Stevie and me.

On Monday, the first day of VBS, Stevie showed up—with his brothers! I saw those boys, and I was countin' candy bars. My dad was pleased too. In the Baptist church, VBS is a church-growth tool. At week's end, pastors sift through registration cards looking for church prospects. A well-timed pastoral visit could mean new families by next Sunday.

Stevie and his brothers came Tuesday, too, but at that point, I was already busily looking for other new prospects and dreaming of more candy bars. Stevie's regular attendance got me nothing. So when the boys failed to show up on Wednesday, my apathy about their attendance would have continued but for my dad's particularly grim expression.

A disquieting mumble was infecting the VBS teachers. "Did you hear what happened?" they asked each other. Horrifying glances were exchanged. Stevie, his siblings, and their mom were dead. Never allowed close enough to hear exactly what had happened, I only heard "car" and "dead," so I *assumed* I knew the details. But I didn't. That is, not until lunch, when I saw the newspaper my dad must have dropped in nauseated horror during breakfast.

The front page featured four school pictures of Stevie and his siblings. The paper had momentarily shifted its coverage from the Vietnam War to the war on Twenty-first Street. The story told of a mother and children who shared the abusive marks of a drunken husband. When the dad abandoned them and left them destitute, they felt a hurt that far exceeded the Maker's specification for the human soul.

The paper described how the mom drugged the children and carried them to the inviting warmth of their running car. In a closed garage, she strung a garden hose from the tailpipe to the car's cabin and ushered her children into a final sleep.

I put the paper down without finishing my lunch. The candy bars had lost their appeal.

In the years that followed, my father continued to penitently retell the story. He was never one for shedding preacher tears, but I heard his voice crack in each new congregation as he relived his regret of having almost gone to see the family the very night the mom and kids died. He had intended to stop by after leaving his second job, but he was just too tired.

Each time he told the story, he would confess to having noticed suspicious marks on the boys; he would tell of hearing neighborhood gossip about the abusing husband. In telling the story, he challenged his listeners at each new congregation to find the pain that existed in the shadow of every church.

I didn't really know the family. Stevie wasn't the boy's real name. I can almost remember his real name but not quite. If my dad were alive, I'm sure he could tell you. He never forgot it because of that one final *almost* of the evening. My dad came to know the family well—posthumously.

The day I wrote this story, I happened to notice a news item buried deep in the national section of the newspaper. It was the story of a mobile-home fire in Mississippi that killed six children. The fire started at 1:43 a.m. in a home lighted by candles; there was no running water, no electricity, no adult supervision for the children ages four months to twelve years.

Reading the story, I thought of Stevie and couldn't help wondering about those Mississippi children. *How close was someone to almost helping them?*

GRIEF COMES TO THE GRIEF COUNSELOR

It's a terrifying and morbid thought, but in my line of work it's sometimes impossible to keep it at bay: I've wondered what I might do if one of my children were killed. I've wondered if I could somehow miraculously remain a minister and comfort those who were also grieving horrific losses? I'm grateful I haven't had to endure that experience, but I still wonder.

I'm sure my friend Sue Wintz wondered too. Like most of us who serve as pediatric chaplains, Sue has long known the meaning of the scriptural admonition foretelling the "rain on the just and on the unjust" (Matthew 5:45 NKJV), but somehow she'd always managed to carry a good umbrella.

Then, on December 2, 2003, Sue's seventeen-year-old daughter, Sarah, was killed in a car accident. As they struggled to survive this unimaginable blow, Sue talked to me about the ways she and her minister husband, Mike, have learned to better align their professional roles with the lessons they've learned from losing a child.

In the days and weeks after the accident, Sue said, "We didn't sleep or eat; we felt like we were in a fog. I had absolutely no idea how deep and dark the hole of parental grief would be."

Yet despite the fog, the Wintz family knew, from her professional perspective, that their "feelings were normal and OK," she said. But the heartbreaking ordeal also demonstrated to her that some professionals "just don't get it sometimes." In fact, a day after the accident, one colleague told her, "You aren't reacting very professionally."

Some even told the Wintzes their grief should be "over" in a matter of months, and soon those acquaintances stopped mentioning Sarah by name. Unbelievably, one colleague even told Sue, "The 'honeymoon year' is over, so you should move on." Sue described these people as "toxic" and noted that grieving parents become very adept at recognizing the ones who are helpful "and the ones who should be avoided."

Gradually Sue has regained some of her former confidence. "I was a good chaplain before my daughter's death," she said, "but through our experience I've learned some things that did and didn't help."

Twenty-five days after Sarah's death, Sue listed those things in her journal. And now, she's asked me to share part of that list with you.

Helped: People who checked on us without an agenda and took care of details like answering our phone, keeping lists of what people brought, cleaning our house, and making sure our cars were running well.

Didn't help: Trying to micromanage aspects of our grief by telling me when I needed to eat and rest or take anxiety medications.

Helped: Food brought every other day, beginning the second week of the accident.

Didn't help: So much food brought all at once.

Helped: People telling me, "My child died too. I'm here for you."

Didn't help: People claiming to know how I feel because their father/friend/dog died.

Helped: The hundreds of people who came to the service and our amazing son, who put together the slide show of Sarah's life.

Didn't help: Giving me advice on when I needed—or didn't need—to go through Sarah's room and things.

Helped: Carolers and Secret Santa gifts. Sarah loved Christmas.

Didn't help: Telling me I needed to realize there are also "others having a bad time in their lives right now."

Helped: The people who listened and never told us to stop crying.

Didn't help: Questions asking us who was at fault in the accident.

Helped: Taking me out to lunch and back into the world.

Didn't help: Asking when we're going to get our "lives and work back to normal."

Helped: All the wonderful donations to the memorial scholarship fund, the live plants reminding us of Sarah, and the flowers brought to the site of the accident.

I find it nothing short of miraculous that Sue remains in her job as a pediatric hospital chaplain. She says she finds in that work a gift for sharing with those who have endured similar losses.

She also says she finds a lasting lesson in Thomas Attig's writing about grief and how relationships with loved ones change after their death. Sue adds, "The truth is, it doesn't end; the relationship is miraculously transformed. I knew that concept before Sarah's death, but now it really hits home."

A TOUGH WEEK FOR FATHERS

Before becoming a hospital chaplain, I thought the worst way a father might lose his daughter was if she met some no-good guy from the other side of the country. But of course, in the hospital, I've seen a lot worse ways than that.

One of them came after leaving a conference with a father whose daughter was dying from cancer. The charge nurse detected the subtle moisture in my eyes, and asked, "You OK, Chaplain?"

"Yeah, I think so," I told her. "It's just a little harder when I see the dad cry."

According to news stories I'd been watching that week, a lot of dads out there were crying. It was the week that Laci Peterson's father, Dennis Rocha, had watched his son-in-law,

Scott Peterson, be arraigned for the murder of Laci and her unborn child, and in another city another father learned that blood from his missing daughter had been found in the car of a man suspected in her disappearance. That same week, yet another dad got the tragic news that his daughter had been struck and killed on the sidewalk outside her high school by a drunk driver. One witness to the accident was the son of a chaplain friend who would later tell his father he was standing twenty feet from the girl when she was struck.

At about the same time the hospital dad was getting the hard news about his daughter's terminal cancer, police officers were pulling up to the home of hospital chaplain Sue Wintz and husband, Michael, to tell them their daughter Sarah had been killed in an automobile wreck.

Over the years, I've held on to the comfortable (but totally fictitious) notion that God protects people whose high calling involves the altruistic and idealistic. I wanted to think that as a chaplain I was exempt from getting the kind of news these parents had received. We all want to think we have some special protection, don't we? But during that same week when headlines flashed the tragic news these other parents (some of them chaplains) had been dealt, I became painfully conscious that I enjoyed no such advantage.

My daughter had recently flown to New York and been greeted by some whacko who cracked her windshield with a rock thrown from an overpass. She survived that ordeal, but then, still mindful of all the bad days other fathers were having that week, I felt an extra chill of reality when I heard that New York was socked in with a major blizzard—and I heard nothing from my daughter for three days. Then, ironically, her phone call telling me she was boarding her return flight coincided with the latest news from Homeland Security warning that terrorists might attempt to smuggle bomb-making material in their socks and roll-on deodorant. These factors had all the makings of a really bad day in a really bad week.

Later that evening, my daughter called to pacify my worries and tell me she had made it home safely. She seemed a bit annoyed with my smothering, mothering, and hovering, but she also managed to give me the latest news. It wasn't all that reassuring.

After hanging up the phone, my wife asked, "You OK, honey?"

"I guess so, but I think she'll be going back to New York sometime in the near future."

"Oh?"

"Yup—she now has a boyfriend in the Big Apple."

It's been a tough week for fathers.

REGRETTING A MOMENT . . . FOR A LIFETIME

Most of us have wondered at one time or another how differently a particular situation or conversation might have turned out if we had only managed to say just the right thing. But have you ever wondered how a moment could have been different if you'd have only remained quiet and listened more?

Billy Graham, who at age eighty-six recently announced his retirement from gospel crusade appearances, told of one such experience during an interview with NBC reporter Brian Williams. Rev. Graham may have spoken to more people than any other living person, but he revealed a personal event he still finds troubling. It wasn't something he had said that caused his regret but someone he'd failed to listen to, perhaps calling to mind

Scripture's admonition: "He who has ears to hear, let him hear" (Matthew 11:15 NASB).

According to the NBC Web site, Rev. Graham had spoken at a breakfast gathering where he was seated beside President John Kennedy. In a whispered conversation, the president asked Billy to ride back to the White House with him.

Billy replied, "Mr. President, I'm sick. I have a fever, and I don't think I ought to ride in the car with you and go to the White House. Let me come over some other time."

The president smiled and said OK. Rev. Graham said he never learned what the president wanted to talk about; another opportunity for a private discussion didn't occur before the president was killed a few months later.

Rev. Graham told his interviewer, "That, to me, is a mystery that I would like cleared up when I get to heaven."

Usually when I think back on my previous conversations, I'll busy myself rewriting them in my head, using all the words I *wish* I'd said. Yet in Graham's encounter, when he had the opportunity to privately say anything to the most powerful man in the free world, Graham regrets most missing an opportunity to hear the words of President Kennedy.

Fourteen years ago, I recall such a regret in my life. My father called me on the eve of his sixty-fifth birthday at 6:57 p.m. I know the time because *Star Trek: The Next Generation* came on at 7 p.m. As soon as I recognized Dad's voice, I began wondering how I might talk to him just long enough to satisfy his need for conversation without missing *Starship Enterprise's* adventures in protecting the universe against the latest threatening alien.

At 6:59 p.m., I asked him what he was most looking forward

to about his birthday. He easily answered that he was hopeful about his new career in real estate.

Good question. Good answer. Done.

At 7:02 p.m., I said, "Hey, Dad, can I call you back in an hour? I've got something going on here." (I guess you can call TV "something," although I can't tell you what.)

At 7:03 p.m., we said some quick good-byes, and I scrambled for the remote to turn on the TV, annoyed that I'd missed the crucial introduction of the show.

Thirty-six hours later, there was another phone call. It was my mom, her voice mentally reminding me that I hadn't kept my promise to return Dad's call. "Norris," she said, "your dad's gone."

"Where did he go?" I asked.

Lost in my own world of daily duties and shallow TV shows, I wasn't hearing the euphemism. *Gone* was my mother's way of telling me my father had died shortly after falling asleep on the night of his birthday.

Since then I've had no regrets over what I said to Dad during our last conversation—but endless regrets over not taking the time to listen to him. What more might he have said? Did he have wisdom to share? He didn't call often. So why had he called that particular night?

As Rev. Graham pointed out, I won't know the answers in this life. But with each recollection of that failed conversation, it becomes harder and harder to wait on heaven.

WHEN THE LIGHTS GO OUT

After reading this book, you may wonder how chaplains deal with the pain of what they see. Maybe you've encountered ministers, spiritual advisers, and faith leaders who give the image they live their lives in a bubble—free from problems, temptations, or tragedies. I suppose that's partly why I've written this book: to refute that idealistic image and show you that ministers aren't perfect. I've written stories about my own anxieties, pride, less-than-perfect parenting, and even lust. Yet, of all the personal feelings I share with folks, I think the one that rings true with the most familiarity is depression.

I've struggled with short bouts of depression much of my adult life, but not too long ago, I experienced a bout of it that dimmed my lights for more than a year—at times nearly extinguishing them altogether. The depression, which was triggered by a colleague who had spread some pretty ugly rumors about me, became so deep, there were times when I was unable to do the simplest tasks such as drive or order food from a menu.

I have often likened my feelings during that time to those experienced a few years ago by the men who served on the doomed Russian submarine *Kursk*. After some sort of serious malfunction, their sub sank to the bottom of the Barents Sea, where the 118 crew members waited in the dark, praying for rescue. They penned some desperate messages in those dark hours, and they spent their last gulps of air praying a kind of doublespeak that death would not overtake them—and that the end might be swift.

Through personal experience, I can tell you that depression can grip your soul and leave you feeling like the men in that boat—believing the whole time in rescue yet at the same time shivering with hopelessness. The fright becomes not so much about dying as it is the terrifying thought that this miserable existence is what living will be like from here on out.

Even so-called mild depression can seem like a thick fog, hiding the formidable presence of the unknown. Like fog, depression swallows everything in its path, menacingly implying that nothing exists it cannot swallow. It will lie to you and tell you the sun will be no more. Like a tulle curtain sweeping across the horizon, it attempts to transform the relevant into shapeless voids.

It would be anachronistic to apply modern psychological terms to the New Testament, but I do believe Scripture suggests that Jesus experienced some pretty depressing moments. He wept about the loss of his friend and felt overwhelming disappointment with his disciples' lack of vigilant prayer. And from the cross, his splintered cry for the future care of his mother reflected the hopeless battlefield cry of a dying soldier for his mom. The Bible says his overwhelming burden for his people caused the stage of Calvary to go dark for three hours.

My trip out of this murky misery and back into healthy air began with an admission that I was overwhelmed and needed help. It took some time, but with the help of family, friends, pastoral supervisors, counseling, and clinical intervention, I found my way out. Of course, there still are days when I attempt to replay some old tapes and find myself staring into an approaching fog bank. On those days when depression returns with a cold sweat in my soul like a recurring case of malaria, I know it is time to re-enact my previously successful strategy: I use prayer to center myself and reach outside the limits of my own needs. I surround myself with those who are able to affirm my calling, hear my heart, and grant me grace. And I am forever grateful that, with God's help, the fog lifts.

WHAT LEGACY WILL YOU LEAVE?

I did something drastic last week. I called my cable company and told them, "Disconnect the cable. Let me hear the silence please."

Apparently, though, the desire to end my relationship with my TV isn't a mutual feeling. It has now become my stalker. In the pediatrician's office, it wails out a nonstop infomercial about weight loss. In the grocery store, it stands atop the end caps, hawking the latest cleanser. And on a perch above the gas pump, it pontificates the wisdom of buying good rain tires, immersing me with the message, "Buy, buy, buy!" It's the mantra of a marketing world where the word *miracle* is defined by how quickly our plants grow or how white our teeth get.

Yet my experience in the hospital reminds me that I do not need TV, I do not need more "stuff," and whatever I do buy may one day be carried away in things like plastic garbage bags by family members who have no appreciation for it.

In a scenario that plays out nearly every day, I see the role of this plastic bag at the end of life. The scene is like this:

The hospital intercom squawks, "Code blue, five north. Code blue, five north." The announcement means someone has quit breathing and requires all the resources of the hospital, including the chaplain.

I scamper down a side stairway and break through the ICU's swinging doors not far behind a respiratory therapist hurriedly pushing a cart stocked with lifesaving equipment and supplies. As the resuscitation team members take their place inside the room, I stand beside a frantic family member.

Despite what you see on TV, resuscitation most often fails. So, in most cases, there soon comes a point when the doctor decides to "call the code," which means he or she pronounces the patient dead.

I spend the next moments with the family in closing rituals and prayers. And as difficult as this is, eventually there comes a more awkward moment. This is the moment the loved ones turn their attention to packing the patient's hospital-room belongings. Families who are not eager to spend another minute in the hospital will often reach for the quickest thing available to pack up the stuff. Often it's a store's plastic grocery bag or even a trash bag.

As I watch the family leave amid the background drone of yet another TV pitch, I often wonder what it might be like when my time comes. Will the bag of stuff my family carries away be filled with things TV persuaded me to buy?

Oh, how I hope that, instead of *stuff*, they take with them a piece of my faith journey that inspires them for other tasks!

It's been said that God doesn't have grandchildren, only children, meaning a person must have his or her own faith, not faith that is passed on by parents. However, it's still a legitimate part of my faith journey to regularly ask myself questions like, *Will there be a part of myself worth commending to my children? What part of me do I wish they would become? And what part of me will die with me?*

I guess all those questions point to the supreme question asked by Jesus: "What profit is it to a man if he gains the whole world, and loses his own soul?" (Matthew 16:26 NKJV).

The answers to those kinds of questions don't often tumble from the TV speakers. And they will certainly never be found at the bottom of a plastic bag filled with possessions.